THE
INSULT
DICTIONARY

THE
INSULT
DICTIONARY

HISTORY'S BEST SLIGHTS, STREET TALK, AND SLANG

Julie Tibbott

Reader's Digest

A READER'S DIGEST BOOK

Copyright © 2013
powerHouse Packaging & Supply, Inc.

Library of Congress Cataloging-in-Publication Data
Tibbott, Julie, 1978-
The Insult Dictionary :
History's Best Slights, Street Talk, And Slang / Julie Tibbott.
pages cm
ISBN 978-1-62145-066-5 (alk. paper) ISBN 978-1-62145-067-2 (epub)
1. English language--Obscene words--Dictionaries.
2. English language--Slang--Dictionaries. 3. Invective--Dictionaries. I. Title.
PE3721T55 2013
417'.2--dc23
2012044236

Design by J. Longo

We are committed to both the quality of our
products and the service we provide to our customers.
We value your comments, so please feel free to contact us.

The Reader's Digest Association, Inc.
Adult Trade Publishing
44 South Broadway
White Plains, NY 10601

For more Reader's Digest products and information,
visit our website:

www.rd.com (in the United States)
www.readersdigest.ca (in Canada)

Printed in China

1 3 5 7 9 10 8 6 4 2

Produced by

PH P&S

YOU'D HAVE TO BE **BARMY** TO KEEP A PET TIGER.

MY MOTHER AND HER **FACE-STRETCHER** FRIENDS GOT BOTOX TREATMENTS.

I'VE GOT A CRUSH ON THAT CUTE **BUNCH OF CALICO.**

It's, like, whatever . . .

Are you tired of today's lackadaisical lingo? Try slipping some vintage slang into your vocabulary. Since the beginning of language, there has been slang—informal words and phrases utilized by certain cultural groups to show they're in the know. Many slang terms have become less taboo with time and are now legitimate parts of the English language, but others have been largely forgotten. In these pages, you'll find plenty of obscure, indelicate terms from times past to titillate your friends and enemies. Just don't blame us if it comes to fisticuffs.

LEMON SQUARES ARE MY ACHILLES' HEEL!
I WOULDN'T PURSUE HER, SHE'S A DELICATAE.
HE'S NO ADONIS, THAT'S FOR SURE.

Ancient Appellations

The ancient Greeks and Romans built the foundations of Western civilization, and their language forms the basis of many of our words and phrases. The Greek and Roman divinities in particular inspired much terminology. In any century, calling upon the gods constituted strong language. Read on for some ancient attitude.

Achilles Ancient Greek warrior, hero of Troy; central figure in Homer's *Iliad.* He was invincible save for one small spot near his heel—hence, an *Achilles' heel* is a person's one assailable weakness.
Achilles' heel, Achilles tendon.

Adonis Greek god of beauty and desire.
That guy is so hot, a real Adonis.

Amazon A member of a race of mythical female warriors.
The roller derby girls are such Amazons.

Ambrosia Food and drink of the gods thought to convey immortality.
That wine is divine, like ambrosia.

Aphrodite Greek goddess of love.
Aphrodisiac.

Arachne A Greek maiden transformed by a jealous Athena into a spider.
Spiders are members of the Arachnid family.

Arcadia Arcadia is the rustic central mountainous region of Greece's Peloponnese peninsula, celebrated by the bucolic poets. *Arcadian* refers to any place or time signifying the simple, rustic, pastoral life of a golden age lost.

Atlas A Greek Titan condemned by Zeus to forever hold the world on his shoulders. A book of maps.

Aurora The Roman goddess of the dawn.
Aurora australis, aurora borealis, auroral, aurorian.

Bacchus Roman god of wine.
When the champagne fountain erupted, the party turned into a wild bacchanal.

. . . .

Boreas The Greek god of the north wind, who has given us the adjective *boreal,* which means "northern."
The aurora borealis lit up the north sky.

. . . .

Calliope Greek muse of heroic poetry. Also the name of a keyboard musical instrument resembling an organ and consisting of a series of whistles sounded by steam or compressed air.

. . . .

Calypso A sea nymph in Homer's *Odyssey* who keeps Odysseus seven years on the island of Ogygia. *Calypso music* originated on the islands of the West Indies.

Cerberus The three-headed hound of the underworld, who stood guard at the gates of Hades and prevented trespassers from entering.
Cerebrum, cerebral, cerebellum.

. . . .

Ceres Roman goddess of agriculture, grain, and fertility.
Cereal, increase.

. . . .

Chaos In Greek mythology, the first beings; a formless void from which the universe was born. All creation, including the first gods, came from Chaos, who was the starting point of everything. Currently means a state of confusion.
It was chaotic in the parking lot after the game, with cars driving every which way.

SAVAGE SAGES

Ancient Greek and Roman writers often mused upon morality in their writings. A selection of pithy lines from some great poets and playwrights shows that they could also be biting in their criticism. These lines reveal that while times may change, the larger moral questions of human life do not.

"We are all clever enough at envying a famous man while he is yet alive and at praising him when he is dead."
—*MIMNERMUS, C. 7TH CENTURY BCE*

"One that hath wine as a chain about his wits, such a one lives no life at all."
—*AESCHYLUS, C. 6TH CENTURY BCE*

"He who mistrusts most should be trusted least."
—*THEOGNIS OF MEGARA, 6TH CENTURY BCE*

"No human thing is of serious importance."
—*PLATO, C. 4TH CENTURY BCE*

"Talk sense to a fool and he calls you foolish."
—*EURIPIDES, C. 5TH CENTURY BCE*

"I have hardly ever known a mathematician who was capable of reasoning."
—*PLATO, C. 4TH CENTURY BCE*

"I only wish I may see your head stroked down with a slipper."
—*TERENCE, C. 2ND CENTURY BCE*

"Of all animals, the boy is the most unmanageable."
—*PLATO, C. 4TH CENTURY BCE*

"For thee to whom I do good, thou harmest me the most."
—*SAPPHO OF LESBOS, C. 7TH CENTURY BCE*

"How great in number are the like-minded men."
—*PLAUTUS, C. 1ST CENTURY BCE*

Chloris A Greek nymph associated with spring, greenery, and new growth.
Chlorophyll, chlorine.

....

Chronos Ancient Greek personification of time.
Chronology, chronometer, chronic, anachronism, chronicle.

....

Cronus Youngest of the Titans, in Greek mythology Cronus was son of Gaea (earth) and Uranus (sky). Known as Kronos and later as Saturn by the Romans, he was father to Zeus, Poseidon, Hades, Hestia, Demeter, Hera, and Chiron; he was overthrown by Zeus.

....

Clotho Youngest of the three Fates, responsible for spinning the thread of human life.
Cloth, clothes.

Dionysus The Greek God of wine, ecstasy, and ritual madness. Roman counterpart is Bacchus.
From what she could recall, that rave was a Dionysian experience, drinking wine and dancing till dawn.

....

Echo Mountain nymph of Greek mythology who loved the sound of her own voice. While Zeus, the God of Thunder, was enjoying the company other amorous nymphs, Echo would distract Zeus's wife, Hera, by telling her long, amusing stories. Upon discovering this trickery, Hera punished Echo by taking away her voice, leaving her with only the ability to repeat the voice of another.
Echo, echocardiogram, echolalia.

Electra In Greek mythology, the daughter of King Agamemnon and Queen Clytemnestra. Electra and her brother Orestes plotted revenge against their mother and stepfather for the murder of their father. An *Electra complex* is a term for a female's psychotic attachment to her father and hostility toward her mother.

Eros The Greek god of sexual love.
Erotic, erotica, erogenous.

Faunus Roman woodland deity who brought prosperity to farmers and shepherds. He was often depicted with the horns, ears, tail, and sometimes legs of a goat.
Faun, fauna.

Flora A minor Roman goddess of flowers, grain, and the grapevine.
Flora, florist, flowers.

Fortuna Roman goddess of fortune and luck, often shown holding a cornucopia in one hand and a wheel in the other, to signify the rising and falling of an individual's prospects.
Fortunate, wheel of fortune.

Furies A set of three Greek goddesses who presided over acts of vengeance.
Fury, furious.

Gorgon In Greek mythology, the Gorgons were three sisters (Stheno, Euryale, and Medusa, the latter the only mortal of the three) who had living snakes for hair and looked so terrifying that any mortal who gazed into their eyes was turned to stone.

Harmonia The Greek goddess of concord and tranquility.
Harmony, harmonious, harmonica.

O WALLS, YOU HAVE HELD UP SO MUCH TEDIOUS GRAFFITI THAT I AM AMAZED THAT YOU HAVE NOT ALREADY COLLAPSED IN RUIN.

No, that line didn't come from a modern-day city worker weary of cleaning up spray-painted buildings. It's from the ruins of Pompeii, the ancient Roman city that was partially destroyed when Mount Vesuvius erupted in AD 79. The ash and pumice that buried Pompeii preserved many of the vestiges of everyday life, like graffiti (originally in Latin, of course). The following selections were found in various places—brothels and basilicas, baths and barracks. The next time you're in the bathroom at a dive bar, consider what it would say about our culture if those walls were to be read 2,000 years later.

Virgula to her Tertius: You are one horny lad!

Vibius Restitutus slept here alone
and missed his darling Urbana.

Secundus defecated here.

If anyone does not believe in Venus,
they should gaze at my girlfriend.

Secundus says hello to his Prima, wherever she is.
I ask, my mistress, that you love me.

I had sex with the barmaid.

Floronius, privileged soldier of the 7th legion,
was here. The women did not know of his presence.
Only six women came to know, too few for
such a stallion.

Postpone your tiresome quarrels if you can,
or leave and take them home with you.

Once you are dead, you are nothing.

Restitutus has deceived many girls.

Phileros is a eunuch!

Cruel Lagulus, why do you not love me?

Harpy In Greek mythology, the Harpies were winged women who tormented mortals.
My girlfriend is always harping on me to put down the toilet seat.

....

Hector The greatest warrior of the Trojans. Homer portrays him as noble, courtly, and peace-loving, but his name now means to bluster and bully.
Every day at recess, he hectors the smallest kid on the playground.

....

Hera Greeek goddess of marriage, she was both sister and wife of Zeus.
Hero, heroine.

....

Hercules Son of Zeus and the mortal Alcmene, a demigod legendary for his strength.
Moving that piano by yourself would be a herculean task.

Hermaphroditus The child of Greek god Hermes and goddess Aphrodite, a minor deity of bisexuality. According to myth, the water nymph Salmacis saw this remarkably handsome boy bathing in her pool and, overcome by lust, tried to seduce him. When he rejected her, she wrapped herself around the boy until they fused, forming a being of both sexes. A *hermaphrodite* has reproductive organs associated with both male and female genders.

....

Hymen Greek god of marriage, invoked during the wedding ceremony with a song.
Hymn, hymen.

....

Hypnos Greek god of sleep, who had enormous power over mortals.
Hypnosis, hypnotism, hypnotic.

Iris Greek goddess of sea and sky, who is a messenger of the gods and personification of the rainbow.
You can see all the colors of the rainbow in iridescent soap bubbles.

....

Jove The Roman counterpart of Zeus, king of the gods, also known as Jupiter. *"By Jupiter"* or *"By Jove"* were expressions of surprise or pleasure. One who is *jovial* has a cheerful disposition, like those born under the influence of the planet Jupiter.

....

Lethe The river of "forgetfulness" in the underworld. From it souls would drink and forget their experiences upon being reincarnated. *Lethargy* is a state of persistent drowsiness or sluggishness.

Mars Roman god of war. The adjective *martial* means of or pertaining to battle.
There are troops everywhere because the city is under martial law.

....

Matuta A minor Roman deity, the goddess of the dawn. Through French, we have *matinée,* a daytime theatrical performance, and *matins,* morning prayer for monks.

....

Mentor When Odysseus left for the Trojan War, he asked his friend Mentor to take charge of his palace and his son Telemachus. Today, *mentor* means a trusted guardian and teacher.
She was a great mentor, who taught me how to succeed in business.

Mercury Roman equivalent of the Greek Hermes, the fleet-footed messenger of the gods. The silver metallic element *mercury* is also called "quicksilver" because of the nature of its movement. A *mercurial* temperament is unpredictable or changeable.

....

Mnemosyne Greek goddess of memory, and mother of the nine Muses.
Never Eat Soggy Waffles is a mnemonic device for remembering the cardinal directions.

....

Morpheus Greek god of dreams. *Morphine,* an addictive compound of the opium plant, is used as an anesthetic or sedative.

Muse In Greek mythology, the nine Muses are the goddesses of the inspiration of literature, science, and the arts.
Music, museum.

....

Narcissus In Greek mythology, this proud and handsome young man fell in love with his own reflection in the water. Unable to leave the beauty of his reflection, Narcissus died. This is the origin of the term *narcissism,* a pathological attachment to oneself.

....

Nectar The drink of the gods in Greek mythology. *Nectar* has come to mean any refreshing drink, the pure juice of a fruit, or the liquid gathered by bees from the blossoms of flowers, used in making honey.

TAKE THE CAKE When someone wins overwhelmingly, or does something incredible, you might exclaim "Well, that really takes the cake!" It is widely believed that this phrase originated in the southern United States of the 19th century, when African-American slaves took part in strutting competitions called cakewalks. Participants would be judged on their style and the winners were awarded a cake. The phrase may actually have much deeper historical roots.

As early as the 5th century BCE, the Greeks used "take the cake" to mean a prize for a victory. Athenian playwright Aristophanes included a scene in his 405 BCE play *The Frogs* of an all-night drinking bout, in which the one who is last awake is given a cake as a prize:

> *Who keeps awake shall take the cake*
> *And kiss whichever girl he pleases.*

Perhaps not his funniest line, though Aristophanes is known as "The Father of Comedy." The fact that he is still read today—well, that really takes the cake.

Nemesis Greek spirit of divine retribution and righteous anger.

....

Nymph In Greek mythology, nymphs were beautiful, idyllic goddesses of nature who enjoyed singing, dancing, and amorous freedom.
She is so promiscuous, some would call her a nymphomaniac.

....

Oceanus A Titan, deity of the waters.
Ocean, oceanic.

....

Odysseus Greek hero of Homer's epic poem *The Odyssey,* which recounts his ten-year journey home from the Trojan War. An odyssey has come to mean a long, eventful journey.
With so many flights canceled because of the hurricane, our trip home turned into quite an odyssey.

Oedipus Mythical Greek king of Thebes who fulfilled a prophecy that said he would kill his father and marry his mother, bringing disaster on his city and family. In Freudian thought, an *Oedipus Complex* describes a male child's possessive feelings for his mother and hostility to his father.

....

Olympus The mountainous abode of the Greek gods.
The Olympics, Olympian.

....

Pan The mischievous Greek god of nature. When travelers were walking the lonely stretches of road between Greek city-states, Pan would surprise them by gently rustling the bushes. His noises inspired the travelers to sudden anxiety, the feeling we now know as *panic.*

Panacea Minor Greek goddess of healing. Her name means "cure for all ailments."
My grandmother thinks chicken soup is a panacea.

....

Pandora In Greek mythology, she was the first woman, carved out of clay and given unique gifts by the gods. She also had a box filled with all the evils of mankind, which were released upon the world when she opened it. Today, a *Pandora's box* is a source of troubles.

....

Pluto Roman god of the underworld.
Plutonium, Pluto.

....

Priapus A minor rustic fertility god of Greek myth, protector of livestock, fruit plants, gardens, and male genitalia. This gave rise to the medical term *priapism,* a painful condition of prolonged erection.

Prometheus Greek Titan credited with creating mankind out of clay and bestowing the gift of fire upon mortals, thus lifting them from savagery to civilization. Something characterized as *promethean* is audaciously original or creative.

....

Psyche The deification of the human soul in Greek mythology.
Psychology, psychiatry, psychoanalysis, psychotic.

....

Python In Greek mythology, the serpent who guarded the center of the earth, the site of the oracle of Delphi. This is where the constricting snake gets its name.

....

Saturn Roman god of agriculture, freedom, and time.
Saturn, saturnine, Saturday.

THE WORLD'S OLDEST PROFESSION
In ancient Rome, prostitution was legal, and there was a great variety of prostitutes at all levels of society. The most reputable ones registered with a government agency called the *aediles*, which issued licenses to and collected taxes from sex workers. The Romans even had a festival for prostitutes, Floralia, dedicated to Flora, the goddess of flowers and vegetation. This springtime celebration symbolized the renewal of the cycle of life and was marked with dancing, drinking, flowers, and wearing colorful clothing.

However, just because prostitution was socially acceptable and somewhat regulated didn't mean that exploitation wasn't a problem. One reason this trade thrived was because Roman soldiers were not allowed to marry and therefore utilized prostitutes not only for sex but for other domestic duties. Many slaves and abandoned children were forced into prostitution.

AELICARIAE
Bakery girls—some flour mills also set up as brothels and even sold phallus-shaped cakes.

AMICA
A female prostitute who provided services to only female clients.

AMBUBIAE
Singing girls who were also prostitutes.

BUSTURIAE
Prostitutes who frequented funerals to service mourners.

CITHARISTRIAE
Harp players who were also prostitutes.

COPAE
A barmaid or tavern keeper who was also a prostitute. This is where the word "copulation" comes from.

CYMBALISTRIAE
These street performers, cymbal players, were also almost invariably prostitutes.

DELICATAE
Kept women of wealthy and prominent men, known as hetairai in Greek.

DORIS
Prostitutes known for their great beauty and lack of clothing.

FORARIAE
Country girls who walked the roads seeking work.

LENA
The proprietess of a brothel.

LENO
A pimp.

LUPAE
Prostitutes who frequented the woods were known as lupae, or she-wolves, possibly because of a wolflike cry they uttered during sex.

MIMAE
Mime players were often prostitutes. Mimae could be seen performing at the Floralia festival.

NOCTILUAE
Prostitutes who worked at night.

SCORTA ERRATICA
A prostitute who walked the streets.

SCORTUM
A male prostitute.

Sirens These half-woman, half-bird creatures lived on a rocky island and sang such enticing songs that seafarers were lured to their death. A *siren* has come to mean a seductive woman or a device that emits a warning sound.

....

Sisyphus An Ancient Greek king whose crimes caused him to be condemned to roll an enormous rock up a hill only to have it roll back down repeatedly. A *Sisyphean* task is one that is difficult and endless.

....

Somnus Roman god of sleep.
Insomnia, somnambulate.

....

Syrinx In Greek mythology, a chaste nymph who rejected the affections of the god Pan and was turned into a bed of reeds, from which Pan then fashioned his first set of pipes. *Syringe* is derived from her name.

Tantalus A man who offended the gods so deeply he was condemned to spend eternity in Hades, where he was made to stand in a pool of water with a fruit tree overhead, which moved out of his grasp whenever he reached for it.
I'm on a diet, but that ice cream is so tantalizing.

....

Titan One of a race of giant deities descended from Gaia and Uranus and from whom were born the Olympian gods and goddesses.
Titanic, titanium.

....

Venus Roman goddess of love, beauty, sex, fertility, prosperity, and victory, counterpart of Greek Aphrodite.
Venereal, venery, veneration.

Vesta Virginal Roman goddess of the hearth, home, and family.
Vested, invest, divest.

....

Vulcan The deity of fire and blacksmith of the Roman gods. His forge was located in various places, but most often under Mt. Etna in Sicily, or similar *volcanic* regions, which betrayed its presence.
Volcanic, vulcanize.

Zephyrus Greek god of the west wind, which signals the return of spring. Today a *zephyr* is a gentle breeze.

....

Zeus Leader of the Olympian gods, son of Cronus and Rhea, often-straying husband of Hera, Zeus wielded the thunderbolt. His Roman counterpart was Jupiter, also known as Jove.

WITH A GRAIN OF SALT This phrase comes from ancient Roman author Pliny the Elder's *Naturalis Historia,* which included a recipe for an antidote to a poison, in which one of the ingredients was salt. A person who ingested a grain of salt would be protected from the effects of the poison. So, if you are skeptical about a threat (hopefully not deadly), you, too, may take it "with a grain of salt," or not too seriously.

HA! MADE YA BLENCH!
THAT GAMESTER KNOWS EVERY LAG IN TOWN!
SHE IS CHILDING —FOR THE FOURTH TIME!

Mockery From the Middle Ages

It may be the favored setting for fantasies featuring dragons, unicorns, wizards, and the like, but for most people, life in the Medieval and Renaissance eras was anything but a fairy tale. It was a time of famine, plagues, and religious and social upheaval. These brutal, squalid conditions made for plenty of salty slang that would make any damsel in distress blush.

abbess *n* the mistress of a brothel.

afeard *adj* afraid.

alder-liefest *adj* most loved.

angling for farthings *v* begging out of a prison window with a cap, or box, let down at the end of a long string.

argentine *n* silver.

atomy *n* a tiny particle; a skeletal person.
You've got to put on weight; you look like a bony little atomy.

balderdash *n* originally, a mishmash of beverages; ultimately a mishmash of words; nonsense.

bantling *n* a young child.

basta *v* enough; stop.
I'm sick of hearing about your hemorrhoids. Basta!

bat-fowling *v* catching birds with a net by night.

bear-garden jaw *n* rude, vulgar language, such as was used at the bear-gardens (arenas or pits used for bear fighting and other "animal entertainments").

beshrew *v* to put a curse on.
That evil sorcerer has beshrewed me!

blackguard *n* a low person; a scoundrel.

blench *v* to flinch.
She opened the fridge and blenched at the sight of the moldy leftovers.

AT SIXES AND SEVENS To be at sixes and sevens is to be in a state of confusion or disorder. If you've ever observed a game of Craps without knowing the rules, you might relate to this feeling—which is appropriate, since Craps is derived from an old game of dice called Hazard, which is where this expression probably came from. In Hazard, one's chances of winning were controlled by a set of rather arbitrary and complicated rules. The most risky numbers to shoot for were five and six, so only careless people "set on cinque and sice" with large amounts of money at stake. In time, the pronunciation of the French numerals changed as they were used by people who misheard the words or did not know the language. The link with the dice game must by then have been severed, or perhaps it was a joke, as seven is an impossible number to throw with one die. The change may also be linked to the sum of six and seven being thirteen, long considered unlucky.

bodkin *n* a small dagger.
The spy hid a bodkin in her blouse.

bootless *adj* useless, unprofitable.
We're never going to make any money at this bootless lemonade stand.

breedbate *n* one who is quarrelsome.

bully-rook *n* a bragging cheater.
That card-counting bully-rook can't shut up about all the money he's won in blackjack.

bum-barrell *n* a padded roll tied around the waist to hold out a skirt.

candle-wasters *n* people who stay up all night drinking.
Those candle-wasters didn't leave the bar till last call.

canterbury story *n* a long, roundabout tale.

childing *adj* pregnant.
She is childling—for the fourth time!

chuck *n* a chicken—used as a term of endearment.

churl *n* a low-born person; a stingy or morose person.

clack-dish *n* collection dish used by a beggar.

cock-shut time *n* twilight, the time of day when cocks and hens go to roost.
Its cock-shut time, boss—if you want me to stay later, you'll have to pay me overtime.

cony-catching *v* poaching, pilfering.

corky *adj* dry, like a cork.

cotton *v* to like, adhere to, or agree with a person.
That guy will cotton to anything I say if he thinks it will get him a date.

court holy water *n* empty words; insincere flattery.

coxcomb *n* a conceited or foolish person.

craven *adj* fainthearted or spineless.

crestless *adj* lowborn; not entitled to bear arms.

cur *n* a mutt or stray dog, or a surly or cowardly fellow.
When confronted with a task that called for courage, he ran away, that craven cur!

custard-coffin *n* the pastry or crust of a custard pie.
That custard-coffin was tasty but it went straight to my hips.

dearn *adj* lonely, solitary.
He was a dearn fellow after his girlfriend moved out.

discase *v* to undress.

doolally *adj* out of one's mind; crazy.
I don't care how healthy kombucha is—you must be doolally if you think I'm drinking that fungus.

drabbing *v* seeking the company of prostitutes.

emulous *adj* jealous.
He felt deeply emulous when he saw his brother's new sports car.

OUCH!

In medieval times, torture was used as a means of extracting confessions and punishing heretics. And they got horribly creative with the tools they used to get the job done.

The **Judas Cradle** was a pyramid-shaped seat over which a harnessed victim was lowered. The victim was tortured by intense pressure and stretching of the orifice, and was often impaled.

The **Pear of Anguish** was an instrument with a pear-shaped metal body divided into spoonlike segments that could be spread apart by turning a screw. It could be used either to prevent people from speaking or as an instrument of torture. The instrument was inserted into the victim's mouth, and then slowly spread apart as the screw was turned.

The **Drunkard's Cloak** was actually a barrel, into the top of which a hole was made for the head to pass through. Two smaller holes in the sides were cut for the arms. A drunk and disorderly person could be punished by being made to put on the uncomfortable "cloak" and walk through town.

The **Rack** was a wooden frame slightly raised from the ground. A victim's legs were fastened to a fixed bar at one end, and his or her hands were fastened to a moveable bar at the other end. The torturer turned a handle, causing ropes to pull the victim's arms until limbs were dislocated or even torn off.

The **Scavenger's Daughter** was a metal frame shaped like an "A" that wrapped around its victim's neck and knees. When tightened, the victim's neck was brought closer to the knees, forcing a kneeling position that resembled scavenging. Eventually, the agonizing compression of the body against itself cut off circulation to the head.

The **Lead Sprinkler** was a wand with a hollow ball at the end. Tiny holes ventilated the ball, which allowed molten lead, hot oil, tar, or any hot liquid to be contained within and "sprinkled" onto its victim with a flick of the wrist, causing scorching burns.

A **Cat o' Nine Tails** was a whip made up of leather thongs knotted at the ends and sometimes fitted with metal spikes to tear the flesh of the victim.

englut *v* to devour ravenously.

eyne *n* eyes.

facinorous *adj* extremely wicked.

fain *adj* happily; gladly.

farced *adj* stuffed.
We englutted every dish on the menu till we were totally farced.

fart catcher *n* a valet or footman who walks behind his master or mistress.

fartuous *adj* falsely virtuous.
That teacher's pet is completely fartuous—she totally cheated on the test.

foreslow *v* to delay; obstruct.

frippery *n* a place where old clothes are sold.
She got an awesome vintage dress at the frippery.

gamester *n* a frolicsome, playful person; a loose woman.

garboil *n* uproar, turmoil.

garderobe *n* privy; toilet.

geck *n* a fool; an object of scorn.

give the fig *v* to insult.
How dare you give the fig to my wife!

goatish *adj* lecherous.

gorbellied *adj* corpulent; with a protruding belly.
He used to be really gorbellied till he went on that diet.

hedge-born *adj* of low birth.

horeson *n* son of a prostitute.

hue and cry a shout given to alert townspeople of the need to chase a fleeing criminal.

irregulous *adj* lawless, licentious.

kicksy-wicksy *adj* restless.
After a long day of studying, she felt suddenly kicksy-wicksy.

knotty-pated *adj* stupid.

laced-mutton *n* a courtesan.

lag *n* a low person.

lass-lorn *adj* dumped by a woman.

leech *n* a physician.
That knotty-pated leech prescribed the wrong medicine—what a stupid geck!

lewdster *n* a lewd person.

loblolly *n* gruel or porridge eaten by sailors.

lumpish *adj* tediously dull.

lunes *n* a fit of mania or madness.
When the tranquilizers wore off, he had a lunes.

mammering *v* wavering, hesitating; stammering.
King George VI was prone to mammering.

meazel *n* a leper.

HOLY ROLLER vs. ROSARY RATTLER

HOLY ROLLER vs. ROSARY RATTLER The Catholic Church was once the dominant religious authority in Western Europe, but by the sixteenth century many folks had grown disillusioned, as it turned a blind eye to abuses such as the rich buying forgiveness for their sins and supposedly celibate clergymen fathering children. Reformers such as Martin Luther, John Calvin, and King Henry the VIII of England were key players in exposing Catholic corruption and popularizing new Protestant denominations (though it could be argued that Henry was more concerned with divorcing his wife so he could marry his mistress than he was about religious doctrine). As the Reformation proceeded, there was a lot of hostility and violence between Catholics and Protestants, which led to many disparaging new terms. These derogatory terms were not all coined during the Reformation, and many, unfortunately, are used in the present day.

CATHOLIC

BOX-TALKER
*In reference to the
confessional booth.*

FISH EATER
*Referring to the old custom of
abstaining from meat on Fridays.*

CRAW-THUMPER
*So called due to the practice
of beating one's breast in
repentance or remorse.*

MACKEREL-SNAPPER
*Another reference to the eating
of fish on Fridays.*

MICK
Referring to an Irish Catholic surname.

ROMISH
In reference to Rome, the center of the Catholic Church.

PAPIST
An old-fashioned term for a follower of the Pope.

ROSARY RATTLER
A reference to the sound of the beads of the Rosary.

PROTESTANT

BILLY BOY
From a song associated with a Protestant street gang.

ORANGIE
An abbreviation of Orangeman, or a supporter of William of Orange, who was Protestant.

CROP
Referring to a historical Presbyterian practice of cutting the hair close to the head using a bowl for guidance.

PRODDY
Sometimes shortened to "Prod," a variation on Protestant.

TUB-THUMPER
A pulpit-pounding preacher or his follower.

HOLY ROLLER
From those who rolled on the floor when overtaken by religious ecstasy.

WASP
Acronym for White Anglo-Saxon Protestant, a group seen as excessively privileged.

mew up *v* to imprison or shut in; to confine.

....

mistempered *adj* deranged; angry.

....

nayward *n* negative; pessimistic.
My dad was thinking about letting me borrow the car, but now he's leaning nayward.

....

ninnyhammer *n* a fool or an idiot.

....

od's body *n* an oath or expression of surprise, from "God's bodkin."

....

orgulous *adj* proud.

....

picking *adj* insignificant.

....

pickt-hatch *n* an area of town once known for its many brothels.

plume-plucked *adj* humbled, shamed, dishonored.
She was plume-plucked when she was caught cheating on her hubby.

....

quailing *v* cowering in fear.

....

questrist *n* a pursuer.

....

reeky *adj* strongly unpleasant smelling.

....

rivage *n* a coast, shore, or bank.

....

roynish *adj* scabby.

....

rubious *adj* red; ruddy.

....

rump-fed *adj* fed on scraps, such as liver, kidneys, chitlings.

ruttish *adj* lustful.
A lot of ruttish couples can be found at that motel during lunch break.

scantling *n* a small amount.

scut *n* a worthless, contemptible person.

sharked *v* snatched up, as a shark does his prey.

shrew *n* an ill-tempered woman.

shrive *v* to confess.

skimble-skamble *adj* rambling, disjointed.

ON TENTERHOOKS To be on tenterhooks is to be anxious, waiting impatiently. But what in the world is a tenterhook? *Tenter* comes from the Latin *tendere,* meaning "to stretch." In the 14th century, the process of making woolen cloth involved stretching lengths of the wet woven material on wooden frames called tenters. The tenter hooks were metal hooks used to hold the cloth in place while it dried. Some old English towns had areas called tenter-fields where many of these racks would have been set up.

"YOU LISP AND WEAR STRANGE SUITS."

You don't earn a reputation as the greatest writer in the English language without knowing how to craft a good insult. Whether tragedies or comedies, the plays of William Shakespeare are peppered with vicious put-downs sure to keep the groundlings at the Globe Theatre entertained. Here are some of the bard's best burns.

"The tartness of his face sours ripe grapes."
CORIOLANUS

"He is deformed, crooked, old and sere; Ill-faced, worse bodied, shapeless everywhere; Vicious, ungentle, foolish, blunt, unkind; Stigmatical in making, worse in mind."
THE COMEDY OF ERRORS

"A foul and pestilent congregation of vapours. What a piece of work is man!"
HAMLET

"Thou crusty batch of nature!"
TROILUS AND CRESSIDA

"Sweep on, you fat and greasy citizens!"
AS YOU LIKE IT

"Why, thou clay brained guts, thou knotty pated fool, thou whoreson obscene greasy tallow catch!"
HENRY IV PART 1

"Away, you cut-purse rascal! you filthy bung, away! By this wine, I'll thrust my knife in your mouldy chaps, and you play the saucy cuttle with me. Away, you bottle-ale rascal! You basket-hilt stale juggler, you!"
HENRY IV, PART 2

"Men from children nothing differ."
MUCH ADO ABOUT NOTHING

"Thou art a boil, a plague sore, an embossed carbuncle in my corrupted blood."
KING LEAR

"Out of my sight! Thou dost infect my eyes."
RICHARD III

slops *n* loose breeches.

small beer *n* a trivial matter.

splice *v* to marry.

spurgall *v* to gall or poke.
Quit spurgalling me or I'm telling Mom and Dad!

stretch *v* to hang.

stuck *v* stabbed with a sword.

swinge-buckler *n* variation of swashbuckler; a wild reveler.
Those swinge-bucklers were partying all night long.

tainture *n* a stain.
That tainture on the shag rug must be from that glass of red wine you spilled, you wretch!

WIDOW'S PEAK Some people's hairlines come to a sharp point on their foreheads, called a widow's peak because it resembles the peak of a hood traditionally worn by women in mourning in the Middle Ages. It is sometimes said that people with such hairlines will become widowed soon after marriage, but since it is an inherited genetic trait, many of those spouses probably lived to pass it along to their children.

termagent *n* a violent diety; an overbearing or aggressive woman.

tilly vally *interj* an exclamation of contempt, used when something is trifling or impertinent.

toggs *n* clothes.

tokens *n* also called "God's Tokens," spots that appear on the chest due to Bubonic plague.

troth-plight *n* a betrothal.

unbarbed *adj* untrimmed.

unbolt *v* to disclose.

varlet *n* a knight's servant; a rascal.

vegetives *n* herbs.

vinewed *adj* moldy.

wailful *adj* lamentable.

wench *n* a lewd woman, a strumpet; *v* to associate with prostitutes.

whey-faced *adj* pallid from fear.

wodecock *n* a person who is not very bright.

wraw *adj* peevish or grouchy.

wretch *n* an unfortunate, unhappy person.

writhled *adj* shriveled, wrinkly.

wroth *adj* intensely angry.

yvel *adj* wicked, mean.

LISTEN UP NICKNINNY!
YOU MISERABLE COUNTRY-PUT BOWYER!
WELL, WELL, WELL! AREN'T YOU THE STIFF-RUMPED TWIDDLE POOP?!

Colonial Cracks

When Europeans began settling in the
Americas and Australia, they brought their
stodgy old languages with them, but they soon
came up with lots of new words inspired
by their "new worlds."

abel-wackets *n* among sailors, blows to the palm of the hand with a twisted handkerchief.

....

actaeon *n* husband to an unfaithful wife.

....

amen curler *n* a priest or cleric. *We need an amen curler to marry us.*

....

ape leader *n* an old maid.

....

apple dumplin' shop *n* a woman's bosom.

....

back biter *n* someone who speaks ill of another behind his back. *As soon as she walked away, that back-biting "friend" started making fun of her shoes.*

backgammon player *n* a homosexual.

....

bail out *v* to leave angrily.

....

balum rancum *n* a naked dance performed by prostitutes.

....

bastardly gullion *n* a bastard's bastard child.

....

baste *v* to beat. *He got thoroughly basted after mouthing off to those bell-swaggers.*

....

bell swagger *n* a noisy bullying fellow.

....

bellwether *n* the chief or leader of a mob.

....

belly plea *n* a female felon's plea of pregnancy, evoked to avoid hanging.

belly timber *n* food of all sorts.
Let's go down to the pizza place and get some belly timber.

....

bird-witted *adj* inconsiderate, thoughtless.
Eating the last donut was a bird-witted move.

....

blind cupid *n* the backside.

....

Blowsabella *n* a woman whose hair is disheveled.
Check out Blowsabella—looks like she just rolled out of bed!

....

bobby *n* a police officer.

....

bobby dangler *n* penis.

....

bog house *n* outhouse; privy.
Are we there yet? I've got to go to the bog house!

bolter *n* an escaped convict who became a bush ranger in Australia.

....

boltsprit *n* nose.
Back off or I'll break your boltsprit.

....

boodle *n* a crowd.

....

bowyer *n* a liar.

....

bracket-faced *adj* unattractive, hard-featured.

....

bran-faced *adj* freckled.

....

buck fitch *n* a lecherous old man.

....

bundling *n* a colonial courtship tradition in which a young man and a woman were allowed to sleep together, each wrapped in a seperate blanket.

WITH THE OLD ALMANACK AND THE OLD YEAR, LEAVE THY OLD VICES, THO' EVER SO DEAR.

American founding father Benjamin Franklin was known for wearing many different hats: those of inventor, scientist, author, postmaster, diplomat, statesman, and philosopher, to name a few. He was also a successful printer in Philadelphia, and in 1733, he began publishing *Poor Richard's Almanack* under the pseudonym Richard Saunders. Almanacs were very popular books in colonial America, utilized for their mixture of seasonal weather forecasts, practical household hints, puzzles, and other amusements. The best-selling *Poor Richard's Almanack* also featured extensive wordplay and sayings that encouraged readers to live by virtues like temperance, frugality, industry, moderation, and chastity. Here are some of Poor Richard's sayings that are still heard from time to time today.

A penny saved is a penny earned.

Light purse, heavy heart.

Necessity never made a good bargain.

To lengthen thy life, lessen thy meals.

No man e'er was glorious, who was not laborious.

If you ride a Horse, sit close and tight,
If you ride a Man, sit easy and light.

Three may keep a secret, if two of them are dead.

An ounce of prevention is worth a pound of cure.

Of learned Fools I have seen ten times ten,
Of unlearned wise men I have seen a hundred.

Wink at small faults; remember thou hast great ones.

Fish and visitors stink in three days.

He that cannot obey, cannot command.

He that would live in peace and at ease,
Must not speak all he knows nor judge all he sees.

An open foe may prove a curse
but a pretended friend is worse.

burnt v to be infected with a venereal disease.
He was consorting with dolly mops and got burnt.

burr n a hanger-on, or dependent.

caboodle n a collection of things.

cackler n a chicken.

cackling farts n eggs.

cap acquaintance n someone with whom one is only slightly acquainted.
Yeah, we may be friends on Facebook, but he's really more of a cap acquaintance.

caperdewsie n the stocks.

Captain Grand n a pretentious man; a braggart.

Captain Standish n the penis.

carrotty-pated adj red-haired.

catarumpus n a riot.
When Justin Bieber appeared at the mall, it caused quite a catarumpus.

cat's foot n a domineering wife.

caudge-pawed adj left-handed.

chaunt v to sing in the streets for money.
Her husband is going to chaunt outside the train station to try and make a few bucks.

chaw bacon n a rube.

cheechako n a newcomer to northern Canada or Alaska; someone dangerously ignorant of the terrain.

chirping merry *adj* tipsy.
After happy hour, we were
chirping merry.

choking oyster *n* a clever answer
that wins an argument.

chuckled-headed *adj* stupid,
thick-headed.

church work *n* any work that
advances slowly.

clout *n* a blow.

clover *n* luxury.
A private plane and a house in the
Hamptons? They sure live in clover.

cock robin *n* a soft, weak person.

collector *n* a bandit or highwayman.

cooler *n* the backside.
Kiss my cooler!

corny-faced *adj* possessed of a very
red, pimpled face.

country put *n* a rube.

cracksman *n* a burglar.

creepers *n* crabs, body lice.

cribbage-faced *adj* scarred by the
smallpox, with pits resembling the
holes in a cribbage-board.

cross patch *n* an ill-tempered
person.

crusty beau *n* one who uses
cosmetics.

curtain lecture *n* a scolding a woman issues to her husband while in bed.
I was trying to sleep, but she insisted on a curtain lecture.

....

cutty-eye *v* to look out of the corners of one's eyes; to leer.
She's been cutty-eyeing me all night.

....

daddles *n* hands.

....

daggletail *n* one whose clothing is spattered with dag (manure) or dirt.

....

dance upon nothing *v* to be hanged.
He danced upon nothing yesterday, today he's in the eternity box.

....

dandy prat *n* a frivolous or trifling fellow.

dark cully *n* a married man with a mistress, whom he visits only at night.
That dark cully has been sneaking out after his wife goes to sleep, hoping to avoid getting caught with his mistress.

....

death's head upon a mop stick *n* a sickly, drawn, emaciated person.

....

devil drawer *n* an untalented painter.
No gallery will ever show that devil drawer's awful paintings.

....

dew beaters *n* feet.

....

dilberry maker *n* the anus.

....

disguised *adj* drunk.

....

dishclout *n* dishcloth.

distracted division *n* husband and wife fighting.

dogsbody *n* someone of no importance.

eternity box *n* a coffin.

face-making *v* begetting children. *The newlyweds are too busy face-making to hang out like we used to.*

Fenians *n* Irish nationalists opposed to British rule.

flash men *n* pimps.

finger post *n* a signpost; a parson, because he points out a way to heaven to others.

flaybottomist *n* a schoolmaster.

flea bite *n* a minor injury.

fossick *v* to steal gold from another digger's claim.

fribble *n* a time-waster; an effeminate fop.

full of emptiness *adj* jocular term for empty. *My bank account is full of emptiness.*

fussock *n* a lazy, obese woman.

fusty lugs *n* a pudgy person. *Better lay off those super-sized soft drinks if you dont want to become a fusty lugs.*

gallied *adj* hurried, vexed.

DEAD MEN TELL NO TALES

The colonial era was also a prime time for piracy. Indeed, the early part of the eighteenth century is sometimes called the golden age of piracy, though it existed long before and well after. As merchant ships plied trade routes across the seas, carrying rich cargoes, *pirates*—otherwise known as *buccaneers, corsairs, freebooters, sea rovers,* and *scallywags*—were often lying in wait upon the high seas, ready to rob these ships of their riches.

A lookout posted in the *crow's nest* of a pirate ship such as a *brigantine,* a *sloop,* a *squarerigger,* or a *schooner* would alert his mateys of the approach of a booty-bearing vessel with a cry of *"Sail ho!"* or *"Avast!"* Then the pirates could attempt to *catch a tartar,* or lure the ship into a trap. By displaying the sinister *Jolly Roger* flag, which identified them as a pirate ship, they might simply frighten the ship under attack sufficiently to let them board.

Once aboard, the pirates searched for *loot* to plunder: exotic spices, fabrics such as silk, gold *doubloons, pieces of eight,* silver, even commodities like flour or wood. Weaponry was prized—a *blunderbuss, cutlass,* or *marlinspike* could do a lot of damage. Prisoners would be given the choice to either jump overboard or join the pirate crew—*walking the plank* probably didn't actually happen very often.

A career in piracy could be ideal if you enjoyed hijacking ships by day and swilling *grog, arrack, bumboo,* or *rumfustian* at night, and didn't mind eating *bilge rats, cackle-fruit, hardtack,* or *salmagundi* for dinner—but it was hard work, too. Pirate crew members had to *swab the deck* daily and *careen,* or remove barnacles and other obstructions from the bottom of the ship so it could move at through the water at top speed to elude lawmen and bounty hunters.

If a pirate failed to do his duties, he could face harsh consequences. *Keelhauling* was a punishment that involved dragging the offender under a ship, across the keel, until near-death or death. And the worst missteps landed the offender in *Davy Jones's locker*—the bottom of the sea. That is, if he wasn't unlucky enough to meet a *sea lawyer,* or shark, first. For all the thrills of pillaging, it's clear that being a *landlubber* was a lot less risky!

A pirate whose exploits were especially daring, ruthless, or lucrative would earn himself (or, occasionally, herself) a colorful nickname: Bartholomew Roberts, a Welshman who grew enormously wealthy from his piracy, was known as *Black Bart.* The fearsome-looking Edward Teach gained the moniker *Blackbeard.* John Rackham's colorful clothing earned him the nickname *Calico Jack.* Sir Henry Morgan, aka *Captain Morgan,* became governor of Jamaica; he also lent his name and legend to a brand of rum. Robert Kidd, known as *Captain Kidd,* was less lucky—hanged for his crimes, he was believed to have left a buried treasure, never found. Olivier Levasseur, *The Buzzard,* was so-called for swiftness of his attacks. Jean Lafitte, who plied the waters of the Gulf of Mexico, was called the *Gentleman Pirate;* he started a pirate colony of his own, and today there is a national historical park in Louisiana that bears his name.

ginger-hackled *adj* redheaded.

gilly gaupus *n* a tall, awkward man.

glass-eyes *n* one who wears eye-glasses.

glimms *n* eyes.

glimsick *n* a candlestick.

gnarler *n* a yappy little dog; a watchdog.
We'd never have known that cracksman was breaking into our home if our gnarler hadn't barked his head off!

gollumpus *n* a bulky, clumsy fellow.

government-men *n* convicts transported to the Australian penal colonies between 1788 and 1852.

grannum's gold *n* hoarded money, originally amassed by the grandmother of the current possessor.
No need for lottery tickets—I'm sitting on grannum's gold!

green gown *n* a romantic tumble on the grass.
He gave her a green gown out on the golf course.

grey mare *n* the better horse; a woman who governs her husband.

grinagog *n* a foolishly grinning person.

grinders *n* teeth.

grumbletonian *n* a discontented person; someone who is always complaining.

gutfoundered *adj* exceedingly hungry.
After a few days on a juice fast, I was gutfoundered.

....

guts and garbage *n* a very fat man or woman; one who has more guts than brains.

....

guzzle guts *n* one greedy for liquor.

....

half seas over *adj* nearly drunk.

....

hang an arse *v* to hang back, to hesitate.

....

hatchet face *n* a long, thin face.

....

heart's ease *n* gin.
That guzzle guts at the bar is already half seas over; no more heart's ease for him!

hell-born babe *n* a lewd youth, one of a wicked disposition.
That hell-born babe threw a dirty diaper at me!

....

hempen widow *n* a woman whose husband was hanged.

....

hoddy doddy, all arse and no body *n* a short, clumsy person.

....

hog grubber *n* a mean or stingy person.

....

hop-o-my-thumb *n* a diminutive person.

....

horn mad *adj* extremely jealous of one's wife; cuckold.
He goes horn mad when his wife wears hot pants to the mall.

INDIGENOUS WORDS As Europeans settled across the New World, words like these from the languages of the native peoples they displaced made their way into the English language.

ANORAK
From the Greenlandic Inuit **annoraaq.**

AVOCADO
From Nahuatl **ahuacatl.**

BAYOU
From the Choctaw **bayuk.**

BILLABONG
From Australian Aboriginal word **bilaban.**

CARIBOU
From Micmac **qalipu.**

CHIPMUNK
From the Ojibwa **ajidamoon,** *meaning "red squirrel."*

COYOTE
From Nahuatl **coyotl.**

HAMMOCK
From Taino, via Spanish **hamaca.**

HICKORY
From the Virginia Algonquian **pocohiquara.**

IGLOO
From the Inuktitut **iglu,** *meaning "house."*

KAYAK
From the Inuktitut **qajaq.**

MOCCASIN
From the Powhatan **mockasin.**

MOOSE
From the Eastern Abenaki **mos.**

MUKLUK
From the Yupic **maklak,** *meaning "bearded seal."*

PAPOOSE
From the Narragansett **papoos,** *meaning "child."*

PECAN
From the Illinois **pakani,** *meaning "nut."*

POWWOW
From the Narragansett **powwaw,** *meaning "shaman."*

SQUASH
From the Narragansett **askútasquash.**

SUCCOTASH
From the Narragansett **msickquatash,** *"boiled corn."*

TEEPEE
From Lakota **thípi,** *meaning "house."*

TOBACCO
Probably from a Carribean Arawakan language, via Spanish: **tabaco.**

TOBOGGAN
From the Micmac **topaghan.**

WALLABY
From the Australian aboriginal word **wolaba.**

ZOMBIE
From West African **zumbi,** *by way of Creole* **zonbi.**

hubble-bubble *n* confusion; a person whose words sound like water bubbling out of a bottle.

Jack Ketch *n* the hangman.

Jerry Sneak *n* a henpecked husband.

join giblets *v* to cohabit as husband and wife without being married; also to copulate.

jolly nob *n* the head.
I'll give you a clout on your jolly nob.

jolter head *n* someone with a large head; a stupid fellow.

kettle of fish *n* perplexed affairs.
He's made a fine kettle of fish of that business deal.

king's pictures *n* coins, money.

knuckle one's wipe *v* to steal someone's handkerchief.

lathy *adj* thin, slender.
She's a lathy wench—she practically disappears when she turns sideways.

lawful blanket *n* a wife.

left-handed wife *n* a concubine.

lenton-jawed *adj* thin-faced, possibly from a too-rigid observation of fasting during Lent.

lickspittle *n* a parasite; tattletale.

linen armorers *n* tailors.

little breeches *n* a little boy.

little clergyman *n* a young chimney sweeper.

loll *n* a mother's favorite child.

long shanks *n* a long-legged person.

long stomach *n* a voracious appetite.

long-tongued *adj* loquacious, not able to keep a secret.
Don't tell him unless you want everyone to know—he's long-tongued.

louse ladder *n* a run in a stocking.

low tide or low water *n* the state of being broke, out of money.

man of the turf *n* a horse racer, or jockey.

marriage music *n* the sounds of children squalling and crying.
Ah, just listen to the sweet marriage music of little Timmy throwing a tantrum.

KICK THE BUCKET To kick the bucket means to die, but why? The bucket in this expression is not a pail, but a yoke or beam from which something can be hung. Animals were hung for slaughter from such a beam, and in their death throes, they "kicked the bucket."

melting moments *n* a couple in amorous congress.

murphies *n* potatoes.

mutton monger *n* a man addicted to sex.

mutton-headed *adj* stupid.

nickninny *n* a simpleton.
You're a nickninny if you noozed to that mutton-munger.

niffy-naffy fellow *n* a trifler.

noozed *v* married or hanged.

nug *n* a term of endearment.

nurse *v* to cheat.
They nursed him out of his inheritance.

nutmegs *n* testicles.

odd-come-shortlys *n* soon.
I haven't had time to clean out the closet, but I'll do it one of these odd-come-shortlys.

owl in an ivy bush *n* a person with big, frizzy hair.

oyster *n* a gob of thick phlegm, spit by a tuberculosis sufferer.

paper skull *n* a thin-skulled person, a fool.

parish bull *n* a chaplain or clergyman.

peppery *adj* warm, passionate.

pin basket *n* the youngest child in a family.

piss prophet *n* a physician who diagnoses his patients solely by the inspection of their urine.

platter-faced *adj* wide-faced.

plug tail *n* the penis.

poisoned: *adj* pregnant. *That wench is poisoned, see how her belly is swelled.*

potato trap *n* the mouth. *Shut your potato trap and give your tongue a holiday.*

prattling box *n* the pulpit.

prime article *n* a good-looking girl. *He started doing yoga hoping to meet a prime article.*

puff guts *n* a fat man.

queer bung *n* an empty wallet. *Losing at the high-stakes poker game left him with a queer bung.*

rattle-pate *n* a volatile talkative person.

receiver general *n* a prostitute.

religious horse *n* a person who prays a lot.

roaring boy *n* a noisy, obstreperous young man.

rum gaggers *n* those who tell exaggerated stories of their adventures at sea.

sammy *adj* foolish; silly.

sapskull *n* one who is simpleminded or sappy.

SAILOR SLANG From the 17th century until World War I, Britain's Royal Navy ruled the seas. Sailor slang was salty and whimsical:

ACKERS
Foreign Currency

ACTING RABBIT
Meat Pie

BANYAN PARTY
Picnic

BILBOES
Leg-irons

BILGE-WATER
Nonsense

BURGOO
Porridge

CHAFFER UP
Tidy

CHOW
Food

CUDDY
Captain's Cabin

FISH EYES
Tapioca Pudding

GIBBY
Spoon

HOG OUT
Clean Up

MUNJY
Food

POZZIE
Jam

SCUPPERED
Dead

SHALLOO
Braggart

save-all *n* a kind of candlestick used by frugal settlers to burn snuffs and the ends of candles.

....

scaly *adj* sordid, foul, base.

....

scandal broth *n* tea.
We discussed all the latest gossip over scandal broth.

scapegallows *n* one who deserves but has narrowly escaped the gallows.

....

scapegrace *n* a wild, licentious young man.

....

school of Venus *n* a bawdy-house or a brothel.

READ THE RIOT ACT If someone reads you the riot act, they're reprimanding you severely. The *Riot Act* was passed in 1715 by the Parliament of Great Britain. It authorized local authorities to declare any group of twelve or more people to be unlawfully assembled and thus obligated to disperse or face punitive action. If the group failed to disperse within an hour of the act being read aloud to them, they could be charged with a felony and possibly put to death.

scragged v hanged.

screw jaws n a person whose face is twisted in an expression of disgust.

sheriff's ball n an execution; a public hanging.

sheriff's journeyman n the hangman.

sitting breeches n overstaying one's welcome.
He's really got his sitting breeches on tonight. Dinner was over three hours ago and he shows no sign of leaving.

slasher n an obnoxious bully.

sluice one's gob v take a hearty drink; assuage thirst.
She sluiced her gob with some freshly squeezed juice.

sly boots n a cunning person.
Old sly boots hid his intentions from us all.

snudge n a thief who hides himself under a bed, in order to rob the house.

soul doctor or **soul driver** n a clergyman.

sparkish adj fashionable.
What a sparkish outfit!

spider-shanked adj thin-legged.

spiritual flesh broker adj a clergyman.

spoil pudding n a priest who preaches long sermons, keeping his congregation in church till the food they left cooking is overdone.

sprained ankle *n* pregnancy. *My neighbor's daughter sprained her ankle—she's due in May.*

squeeze crab *n* a sour-faced person.

stewed quaker *n* burnt rum, with a piece of butter: an early-American remedy for a cold.

stiff-rumped *adj* proud; pretentious.

stomach worm *n* hunger. *It's been hours since I ate, and the stomach worm is gnawing at me.*

strip-me-naked *n* gin.

stub-faced *adj* scarred by smallpox.

sunshine *n* prosperity.

swadkin *n* a soldier.

swag *n* thief's booty; travelers' belongings wrapped up in a roll.

swell *n* a gentleman.

swizzle *n* a drinkmade from spruce beer, rum, and sugar. The 17th regiment had a society called the Swizzle Club, at Fort Ticonderoga in 1760.

tantadlin tart *n* human excrement.

taplash *n* bad beer.

tea voider *n* a chamber pot.

tears of the tankard *n* splashes of beer on a mans clothing.

thornback *n* an unmarried woman, a spinster.
My great-aunt is such a thornback, I'll bet she's never tipped the velvet.

tib *n* a young woman.

tibby *n* a cat.

timber toe *n* a man with a wooden leg.

tip the velvet *v* to kiss with tongues.

to shoot the cat *v* to vomit due to excessive alcohol intake.
He tottered home late, covered in tears of the tankard, then shot the cat.

to snabble *v* to loot or plunder; to kill.

SCUTTLEBUTT Rumors and gossip are sometimes referred to as **scuttlebutt.** This term originally applied to an open cask of water kept on a ship's deck for use by the crew. It comes from scuttle, meaning "to cut a hole in," and butt, meaning "a large cask." Sailors would gather around the cask and trade stories and gossip, much like modern office workers do at the water cooler or coffeepot.

topper *n* a violent blow to the head.

totty-headed *adj* idiotic; hare-brained.

trotters *n* feet.
Get moving, lift those trotters.

trusty trout *n* a true friend.

tune *v* to beat.
Those bullies tuned him badly.

twiddle diddles: *n* testicles.
If he isn't taking the hint, a swift kick to the twiddle diddles will surely get the message across.

twiddle poop *n* a finicky or fussy person.

two thieves beating a rogue *v* batting one's hands against one's sides to keep warm in cold weather.

under the rose *adj* privately or secretly.

unlicked cub *n* an uncouth young person.
Ill-mannered and poorly dressed, the summer intern was an unlicked cub.

venus's curse *n* venereal disease.

vice admiral of the narrow seas *n* A drunken man who urinates under the table on his companions' shoes.

victualling office *n* the stomach.

YANKEE DOODLE During the American Revolution, the Colonists and the British they were rebelling against had no shortage of insults for each other. British soldiers, with their red uniforms, were jeered as **Redcoats, regulars, lobsters, red herring,** and **bloody backs.** And in turn, the British mocked American soldiers with a song called "Yankee Doodle." However, as the Americans began to overtake the British in battle, they claimed the song as their own and began singing it as an anthem to taunt their enemies. The song as we know it today begins:

Yankee Doodle went to town
A-riding on a pony,
Stuck a feather in his cap
And called it macaroni.

That last line has nothing to do with pasta—the Macaroni wig was an extreme fashion in the 1770s and became a slang term for a foppish man. Therefore, the verse implies the Yankees were so unsophisticated that they thought simply sticking a feather in a cap would make them the height of fashion.

They may not have been as stylish as their British foes, but the Americans triumphed in the end, winning independence from the crown. "Yankee Doodle" has been a popular patriotic song ever since.

water bewitched *n* very weak punch or beer.

wear the willow *v* To mourn the loss of a sweetheart.
He's been wearing the willow ever since she dumped him for that other guy.

wet Quaker *n* a member of the Quaker sect who has no objection to drinking wine.

whack *n* a share of ill-gotten gains.

whiddler *n* an informer.
After he got busted by the Feds, the thief turned whiddler.

whipster *n* a smart person.

whisker splitter *n* a spy; someone who dabbles in intrigue.

whither go-ye *n* a wife; so-called because wives tend to question their husbands as to whither they are going.
I'm surprised to see you at the poker game, Bob! How'd you get past your whither go-ye?

windy *adj* foolish; empty headed.
It's a windy girl who succumbs to flattery.

wolf in the stomach *n* a monstrous appetite.

wrapped up in warm flannels *n* having imbibed freely of alcoholic beverages.
Crack open your best vintage and let's get the wet Quaker wrapped up in warm flannels!

wry-neck day *n* hanging day.

Wild West Words

In the 1800s, intrepid seekers of fortune trekked the frontiers of the new world's borders in search of freedom, land, and gold. Not only did they find adventure and make their fortunes, but they also came up with a wealth of new words and colorful expressions. Expand your vocabulary with some of these frontier phrases.

a hog killin' time *adj* an enjoyable pastime.

....

absquatulate *v* to abscond; to make a sudden departure.

....

airin' the lungs *v* cussing.

....

argufy *v* to dispute.

....

backdoor trots *n* diarrhea.
The vittles I ate at the barrel-house gave me the backdoor trots.

....

barking irons *n* pistols.

....

barrel-house *n* a cheap saloon.

....

bay window *n* a protruding abdomen, due to either overeating or pregnancy.
I doubt that dress will fit over this bay window I'm sporting.

bed him down *v* to kill a man.
Don't argufy with that blackleg; he'll bed you down with his barking irons.

....

bib and tucker *n* good clothes.
Put on your best bib and tucker for church.

....

blackleg *n* a gambling cheat.

....

bone orchard *n* cemetery.

....

brumby *n* a bronco.

....

bull cook *n* a male cook or kitchen helper in a logging or mining camp.

....

bulldog *v* to wrestle a steer to the ground so that it may be branded.

....

bunch of calico *n* a girl or woman.
I've got a crush on that cute bunch of calico who works at the coffee shop.

bunco trick *n* a con game.
She fell for his bunco trick and lost her life savings.

California widow *n* a woman deserted by her husband for the California gold rush.

cayuse *n* a horse.

chaser *n* a weaker alcoholic drink that follows another drink.

cow juice *n* milk.

cowboy job *n* a reckless robbery; hold-up staged by amateurs.

cowpuncher *n* a cowboy.

cut dirt *v* to run away.

dab hand *n* an expert.

dead man's hand *n* aces and eights; the hand played by Wild Bill Hickock when he was shot to death.

desert rat *n* an old, grizzled prospector who lives in the desert.

devil's addition *n* a town's red-light district.

devil's tar *n* oil.

dogie *n* a motherless calf.
The kind cowpuncher fed the starving dogie a bottle of milk.

down to the blanket *adj* nearly broke.
I'd love to go out to dinner with you, but that restaurant is pricey, and I'm down to the blanket.

CHOO CHOO CHATTER The railroads built across North America in the 1800s made the West accessible to more settlers who rode the *ironhorses,* or steam trains, across the nation. Here are some commonly used railroad terms of the era.

ASHCAT
Also called a "stoker," this was the locomotive fireman, who kept the train's fire burning.

BAGGAGE SMASHER
A baggage handler.

BAKE-HEAD
A locomotive engineer or locomotive fireman.

BLACK SNAKE
A train made up of coal-carrying cars.

BLIND BAGGAGE
A baggage or mail car with no door.

BOOMER
A railroad worker who changes jobs often.

CINDER CRUNCHER
The flagman.

DANGLER
An express train.

DONIKER
A freight train brakeman.

DOUBLE-HEADER
A train pulled by two engines.

DOUSE THE GLIM
To extinguish the lantern.

GANDY DANCER
*One who lays
railroad tracks.*

GOND
A gondola railroad car.

HIGHBALL
*A lantern signal meaning
"full speed."*

HOG
A large locomotive.

HOGMASTER
The engineer on the train.

KAYDUCER
*A train conductor who
would, for a fee, allow known
gamblers or con men to ply
their trade among passengers.*

LOUSE-CAGE
A railroad caboose; a bunkhouse.

MASTERMIND
Railroad trainmaster.

MUD-CHICKEN
A surveyor.

PINHEAD
The brakeman.

PLUG
A slow passenger train.

POSSUM BELLY
*An extra storage compartment
under a railroad car, sometimes
utilized by train-hopping hobos.*

RAILROAD BIBLE
A deck of cards.

REDBALL
A fast freight train.

SLING MORSE
Operate a telegraph.

dry-gulch v to kill sheep or cattle by stampeding them over a cliff or into a dry gultch; to ambush a person.

dudine n a fashionable woman.

....

duff v to steal cattle.

DIXIE Why is the southern United States called "Dixie"? There are several possible reasons. It may refer to privately issued currency originally from the Citizens State Bank in Louisiana during the American Civil War. These banks issued ten-dollar notes labeled "Dix," French for "ten," on the reverse side. The notes were known as "Dixies" by English-speaking Southerners, and the area around New Orleans and the French-speaking parts of Louisiana came to be known as "Dixieland." Eventually, usage of the term broadened to refer to most of the Southern States. Another possibility is that the word refers to a slave owner named "Mr. Dixy." His rule was so kind that "Dixy's Land" became synonymous with a place abounding with material comforts. Or perhaps the person it refers to is Jeremiah Dixon, a surveyor of the Mason-Dixon line, which defined the border between Maryland and Pennsylvania, known as the dividing line between North and South.

dumpish *adj* sad or depressed.

dust *n* gold dust; money.

dusty butt *n* a short person; one so close to the ground that his butt is always dusty.
Hey, dusty butt, how's the weather down there?

eatin' irons *n* silverware.

euchre *v* to lie or deceive.

flannel mouth *n* a smooth or fancy talker, especially a politician or salesman.
Sensing the cowpuncher was down to the blanket, the rancher acted like a flannel mouth to sell the cayuse.

flea trap *n* a cowboy's bedroll.
I can't find a spot to lay my flea trap.

flip *n* a hot drink of beer, rum, and sugar.

four-flusher *n* a cheater at cards; a bluffer.

fresh fish *n* a gullible person.

funkify *v* to frighten, to alarm.

get a wiggle on *v* hurry up.

get hitched *v* to marry.

give the mitten *v* when a lady turns down a man's proposal or dumps him.

go boil your shirt *v* get out of here; bug off.

go up the flume *v* to die.
That old miner has gone up the flume.

THE FRONTIER ON FILM

A stranger rides into town. The saloon doors swing open. There will be whiskey drinking, long stares from under the Stetson brims, and a brawl or six. Must be a western! Here are some memorable quotes from some great movies of the genre.

"You see, in this world there's two kinds of people,
my friend—those with loaded guns, and
those who dig. You dig."
—*THE GOOD, THE BAD AND THE UGLY* (1966)

"Young fella, if you're looking for trouble,
I'll accommodate ya."
—*TRUE GRIT* (1969)

"When a man is a killer, arsonist, cheat, and
a coward, it's hardly surprising if he turns
out to be a liar as well."
—*BREAKHEART PASS* (1975)

"Yes, it's true you are a good woman.
But then again, you may be the anti-Christ."
—*TOMBSTONE* (1993)

"Why should a man walk around with a pistol, and then let himself be insulted? That's mighty strange."
—*FOR A FEW DOLLARS MORE* (1965)

"When you take the devil into your mouth . . . you're doomed! For he is lying there . . . Waiting for you . . . inside that bottle of whiskey."
—*HANG 'EM HIGH* (1968)

"It's a pretty day for makin' things right!"

"Well, enjoy it, 'cause once it starts, it's gonna be messy like nothing you ever seen."
—*OPEN RANGE* (2003)

"Only problem you have, Sheriff, is a short supply of guts."
—*HIGH PLAINS DRIFTER* (1973)

"I know . . . you have no money. After all, you just got into town. Well if you don't mind doing a little killing you will have no trouble finding someone eager to pay you."
—*A FISTFUL OF DOLLARS* (1964)

goldurn *adj* euphemism for god-damn.

Gone to Texas *v* ran away, often to escape debt. The letters (G.T.T.) were often left scrawled on abandoned houses.

goober *n* peanut.

gospel mill *n* a church.
We're going to the gospel mill to get hitched.

grass widow *n* a divorcée.

grub pile *n* a meal.

grubstake *n* provisions supplied to a prospector in return for a share in the claim.

hatchetman *n* hired killer.

hay burner *n* an old horse.

heifer dust *n* snuff; nonsense.

high-grader *n* a miner who stole big nuggets from the sluice boxes.

hoedown *n* a party that features dancing.

honeyfuggle *v* to flatter; to deceive with sweet talk.
He honeyfuggled her at the hoedown, but she was too smart to fall for such a cad.

hoosegow *n* prison.

jerkwater town *n* a small town primarily known as a place where trains stopped for water.
She left that jerkwater town behind for the big city.

kick up a row *v* to create a disturbance.

lead poisoning *n* the result of being shot.
She died of lead poisoning from a .357 Magnum.

lily liver *n* a coward.

lookin' at a mule's tail *v* plowing.

Mexican strawberries *n* dried beans.

muggins *n* a scoundrel.

mulga *n* rumor.

mysteries *n* sausages, because it was a mystery what they were made of.
They've got mysteries on offer in the cafeteria today.

necktie party *n* a hanging.
Floyd got himself an invitation to a necktie party when he stole that horse.

night hawk *n* the cowboy who had to stay up all night and stand guard while the others slept on a cattle drive.

nobbler *n* glass of spirits.

nose paint *n* whiskey.

old Betsy *n* a favorite gun.
Anticipating trouble, he stuffed old Betsy under his coat.

painted lady *n* a prostitute.

pard *n* a partner or friend.

parlor jumper *n* horse-breaker.

SINGLE WHITE COWBOY

For many men, the western frontier held great promise. There, they might stake their claim on an expanse of fertile land, become successful ranchers, or even strike gold. But what good is all that without someone special to share it with? Unfortunately, in the Wild West, cattle were more plentiful than women. To find a mate, male settlers often advertised in newspapers that would reach the ladies back east, such as *Matrimonial News,* a weekly publication dedicated to "promoting honorable matrimonial engagements and true conjugal facilities" through its personal ads. Women in search of a new life could place ads, too. These mail-order brides were known as "catalogue women."

Courtship was conducted via letters and photos, and most couples agreed to marry before ever meeting each other in person. This could be disastrous, as it was with the woman who found herself at the altar with a man who had robbed her stagecoach only hours before. But many successful matches were made through these ads, too. Hard to imagine for Internet daters, who likely have no more than their pride and the cost of a meal at stake upon their first meeting with a potential love interest!

Personal ads have always had their own lingo. These ads of the old West are blunt about financial arrangements and focus more on practical skills than interests—after all, the harsh life of a pioneer didn't allow much time for piña coladas and getting caught in the rain. Both men and women required a mate who would help them survive, and hopefully thrive, in the territories. With any luck, love and romance would come later. Here are samples of some of the lonley hearts ads.

*Wanted: A girl who will love, honest, true and not sour;
a nice little cooing dove, and willing to work in flour.*

* * *

*I am fat, fair, and 48, 5 feet high. Am a No. 1 lady, well fixed
with no encumbrance. Want an energetic man that has some
means, not under 40 years of age and weight not less than 180. Of
good habits. A Christian gentleman preferred.*

* * *

*A bachelor of 40, good appearance and substantial means,
wants a wife. She must be under 20, amiable and musical.*

* * *

*A lady, 23, tall, fair and good looking, without means,
would like to hear from a gentleman of position wanted a wife.
She is well educated, accomplished, amiable, and affectionate.*

* * *

*Aged 27, height 5 feet 9 inches, dark hair and eyes, considered
handsome by all, his friends united in saying he's amiable and will
make a model husband. The lady must be one in the most extended
acceptation of the word since the advertiser moves in the most
polished and refined society. It is also desirable that she should
have considerable money.*

pelter *n* an inferior or cheap horse.
That pelter ain't good for nothing but glue.

pemmican *n* dried meat.

piece of pudding *n* a piece of luck, a welcome change.

pilgrim *n* a greenhorn; newcomer.

pine top *n* cheap whiskey.

plug *n* a hat, especially a top hat.
Put your plug back on before you get sun stroke.

pokey *n* jail.

popskull *n* moonshine.
He sold his popskull to an undercover rozzer and got sent to the pokey.

pothooks *n* spurs.
Dig yer pothooks into that cayuse, cowpoke!

prairie oysters
or **mountain oysters** *n* fried or roasted calves' testicles.

punching dogies *v* herding cows, or driving the cattle to market.

ratbag *n* a despicable person.

rawheel *n* a tenderfoot.

rode hard and put up wet
adj ugly, rough; or hard looking.
That old horse looks like he's been rode hard and put up wet!

rozzer *n* a police officer.

rube *n* a farmer; a country bumpkin; a rustic.
That rube can't even parallel park.

Sam Hill euphemism for "hell."
What in the Sam Hill are you doing with my wallet?

shank of the evening *n* the latter part of the afternoon.

sheezicks *n* a criminal.

shivaree *n* a noisy party or gathering outside the home of newlweds.

shut-pan *adj* secretive, silent.

six-bits *n* the sum of 75 cents.

skinch *v* to cheat; to take advantage of.

skunk eggs *n* onions.
This marinara needs more skunk eggs.

slumgullion *n* a weak drink; an unappetizing stew.

sockdolager *n* a decisive blow.
The fistfight ended with a powerful, bone-crunching sockdolager.

sod-buster *n* a farmer.

soiled dove *n* a prostitute.

sorehead *n* one who angers easily or complains frequently; one who holds a grudge.
That sorehead always sends his food back at restaurants.

TELEGRAPH TALK The establishment of the first Transcontinental Telegraph system in 1861 allowed almost instantaneous communication across great distances. Within days of its start of operation, this major advance in technology put the Pony Express mail delivery service out of business.

Because senders paid per word on their telegrams, a variety of codes and ciphers were developed to get the message across more efficiently—a bit like the shorthand people use in text messages today, but the sentiments represented by a single word or acronym could be considerably more involved than "OMG."

The following selections are from the 9th edition of the *Adams Cable Codex,* published in 1896. Aimed at travelers and businessmen, this hefty volume cost 50 cents and claimed to save its cost ten times over in one message.

ABASTIS
Am quite ill.
Please come here at once.

ABHORRENCE
Arrange for my return.

ABSCONDING
Business is very bad.

BISCUIT
Please name and reserve room for
married couple and two children.

BUTTON
A matter of great importance.

CALAMITOUS
Acknowledge receipt by mail.

CANINE
Advise you not to do it.

CAPER
Am alone. Where can I meet you?

DAPTIVATE
*An accident, not serious,
has occurred.*

DESTINY
*In absence of advices from you,
am unable to decide what to do.*

DISGORGED
Keep this strictly private.

EFFEMINATE
Shall start at once.

EMOLUMENT
Think you had better not wait.

EXEMPLIFY
*Will you gain anything
by waiting?*

FALSIFY
Your theory is impracticable.

INSOLUBLE
If market goes up, sell.

LANTHANUM
*Is in our opinion a
splendid purchase.*

MADMAN
Why do you not sell?

PALMATE
*Are well known and are
considered perfectly reliable.*

REPINING
*Hope all is going well
with you.*

RESTLESS
Merry Christmas to you all.

SHREWISH
Will sail Sunday.

sourdough *n* an old-timer; a prospector experienced enough to carry bread starter on his person.

spill-quirley *n* a cigarette.

spitbox *n* a spittoon.

spoopsie *n* a silly person.

sprung *adj* drunk.

stancheous *adj* strong-looking.

stiffener *n* an alcoholic drink.
Too much stiffener will make even the most stancheous fellow sprung.

stone-fence *n* cider with whiskey added.

streaky *adj* confused.

stringing a whizzer *v* telling a tall tale.
He strung so many whizzers that he got streaky about what was actually true.

Sunday soldier *n* an unprofessional soldier.

swill-boys *n* a gang of rowdy young men.

take a shute *v* to run away.
I taught my son to take a shute if a stranger makes him uncomfortable.

tangle-foot or tangle-leg *n, adj* cheap whiskey, and the unstable gait that results from drinking too much of it.
He got a bad case of tangle-foot last St. Patrick's Day.

ten commandments *n* fingers or fingernails.

tottlish *adj* unsteady.
She's a tiny thing, one shot of pine top and she's sprung and tottlish.

unmentionables *n* underwear.

unrooster *v* to tame a horse to work after he has wintered on the range.

vamoose *v* make a shift departure.

vaulting house *n* a brothel.
I'm headed to the vaulting house to find me a soiled dove for the evening.

voyageur *n* fur trader who traveled by canoe.

wabash *v* to cheat.

wabble *v* to talk non-stop.

waddie *n* cattle rustler.

wake snakes *v* to make a lot of noise.
She wabbled so loudly, she woke snakes.

wamble-cropped *adj* nauseated.

weak sister *n* an undependable or cowardly man.

wiggle-tall *n* mosquito.
I don't know how that voyageur handles all the wiggle-talls on the water.

wild mare's milk *n* whisky.

yen-yen *n* a desire for opium.

THE COLOR OF THAT **FLESH-BAG** REALLY BRINGS OUT YOUR EYES.

I'M SO **CORNED**, I THINK I'M GOING TO BE SICK.

UH-OH . . . MY **COLLY-WOBBLES** AREN'T FEELING SO WELL AFTER EATING ALL THAT FATTY FOOD.

Victorian Venom

During Queen Victoria's long reign (1837-1901), the middle class grew in size and influence, but lace doilies and propriety didn't stop the Victorians from throwing down. Some of the most memorable phrases of the period were the ones used outside of the drawing room.

apple-pie order *adj* very tidy, in precise order.

Botheration! Your bedroom is an absolute mess. Get this in apple-pie order by the end of the day, or you're grounded!

arm props *n* crutches.

ary *adv* either.

barmy *adj* insane.
You'd have to be barmy to keep a pet tiger.

BATS IN THE BELFRY A crazy or eccentric person might be said to have bats in the belfry. The word "belfry" comes from the Old French *berfroi,* meaning "a wooden siege tower." Over the years, the meaning shifted from a siege tower to a watch tower (which may or may not have had alarm bells), and by the 14th century, a belfry was a bell tower and a church steeple. But it wasn't until the late 19th century that the term "bats in the belfry" was popularized. Since a belfry is a likely place to find bats, the belfry represents the head and brain, and the bats the insane thoughts that are flying around there. You might also just call a person like this "batty."

barnacles *n* a pair of eyeglasses. *If you think that guy is good looking, you'd better put on your barnacles and look again.*

....

bellows *n* the lungs.

....

black diamonds *n* pieces of coal.

....

blarney *n* flattery, exaggeration.

....

blower *n* an informer. *After the thief was caught by the cops, he turned blower on his entire gang.*

....

blue devils *n* feeling of sadness; depression.

....

blue murder *n* a desperate or alarming cry.

....

bonnet *n* a gambling cheat.

botheration! *exc* an exclamation used when one is troubled or annoyed. *Botheration! I wish these telemarketers would stop calling.*

....

bread basket *n* the stomach.

....

brick *n* a person of high character. *What a guy—he's a regular brick.*

....

bumper *n* a full glass or goblet.

....

bunch of fives *n* the hand, or fist.

....

burying a moll *n* breaking up with a girlfriend.

....

buz-napper *n* a young pickpocket. *She hollered blue murder when the buz-napper stole her cell phone.*

....

cagg *v* to abstain from liquor for a length of time.

THE DARK SIDE OF MOTHER GOOSE

Children were once seen as little adults, but this began to change in the Victorian era. Finally, upper and middle class children could enjoy a carefree, innocent time of romping with friends, playing with toys, and reciting silly songs about . . . decapitation and political intrigue? Many traditional nursery rhymes are purported to have deeper, darker meanings behind their sing-song words. The following interpretations are disputed, but they'll certainly make you question how child-friendly Mother Goose really is.

> *Jack and Jill went up the hill*
> *To fetch a pail of water.*
> *Jack fell down and broke his crown,*
> *And Jill came tumbling after.*

This rhyme goes back at least to the 18th century, though Jack and Jill were common-enough names in 16th-century England that they became short for any generic pair of a boy and a girl, and the phrase was used by Shakespeare in A Midsummer Night's Dream: "Jack shall have Jill; nought shall go ill." One theory traces the rhyme back to a Norse myth in which a brother and sister on their way to fetch water are transported to the moon; another explanation links the rhyme to a taxation scheme during the rule of Charles I. Still another version links the story of Jack and Jill to the execution of Louis XVI and Marie Antoinette.

Little Jack Horner
Sat in the corner,
Eating a Christmas pie;
He put in his thumb,
And pulled out a plum,
And said, "What a good boy am I!"

Almost certainly based on a much earlier folktale, this rhyme was well-known by the 18th century. However, in the 19th century the story most commonly associated with the rhyme began to gain currency, when it was postulated that Little Jack may actually have been one Thomas Horner, who was steward to the last abbot of Glastonbury before the dissolution of the monasteries under Henry VIII of England. As the story goes, prior to his abbey's destruction, the abbot sent Horner to London with a huge Christmas pie that had the deeds to a dozen manors hidden within it. During the journey, Horner dug into the pie and took out the deeds of the manor of Mells, which he had his eye on as it included a number of valuable lead mines. The "plum" was thought to be a pun on the Latin plumbum, for lead.

Serious study of Mother Goose and other old folktales and rhymes reveals that most have complicated origins, with elements drawn from different sources, but it is remarkable how easily these popular rhymes could seem to correspond accurately to contemporary events, especially scandals.

catgut scraper *n* a fiddler.

chavy *n* a child.

chicken-hearted *adj* cowardly.

colly-wobbles *n* the bowels.
My colly-wobbles aren't feeling so well after eating all that fatty food.

coopered *adj* worn-out, useless.

corned *adj* drunk.

crabshells *n* shoes.

cracking a kirk *v* breaking into a church or chapel.

crammer *n* a lie, or a person who lies.

dimber damber *adj* very pretty.

divers *n* pickpockets.

do the bunk *v* to run off.
He had to do the bunk after cracking the kirk.

dodger *n* a sneaky person.

doggo *adj* hidden.

dollymop *n* a prostitute.

doss *n* a resting place, a bed.

feathers *n* money, wealth.

fiddle-faddle *n* idle chatter.

flag *n* an apron.

flesh-bag *n* a shirt.
The color of that flesh-bag really brings out your eyes.

gammy *adj* bad, unfavorable, ill-tempered.

gum *n* loud, abusive language.
He was tossed out of the restaurant for giving the gum to the walker.

gutter lane *n* the throat.

hammered for life *adj* married.

herring pond *n* the sea.
The lifeboat could barely stay afloat in the heaving herring pond.

in the twinkling of a bed post in a moment; very quickly.

ivories *n* teeth.
Go and brush your ivories, your breath smells terrible.

knapped *adj* pregnant.

knark *n* a hard-hearted and brutal person.

knife it *v* stop; don't proceed.
Knife it! There's a dead end ahead.

London particular *n* thick London fog.

mill one's nob *v* bump the head or fracture one's skull.
He fell on the ice and milled his knob.

moll tooler *n* a female pickpocket.

nutmeg *v* to deceive or swindle.

nymph of the pave *n* a prostitute.

on the batter *adj* out on the streets, engaging in noisy revelry.

COCKNEY RHYMING SLANG

COCKNEY RHYMING SLANG Originating in London's East End in the mid-1800s, cockney rhyming slang replaces a common word with a rhyming phrase of two or three words and then, in some cases, omits the secondary rhyming word, making the meaning of the phrase elusive to listeners not in the know. For example, to "have a butcher's" means to have a look, from "butcher's hook." It's said that rhyming slang came about as a secret code for London street traders, the costermongers, to conceal their illicit practices from eavesdroppers.

ALIVE OR DEAD
Head

APPLE AND PEARS
Stairs

ARISTOTLE
Bottle

BAKER'S DOZEN
Cousin

BLUE MOON
Spoon

BOYS ON ICE
Lice

BUBBLE AND SQUEAK
Speak

CHEESE AND KISSES
Missus

CLEVER MIKE
Bike

CRUST OF BREAD
Head

CUT AND CARRIED
Married

DUKE OF YORK
Fork

FIELD OF WHEAT
Street

GOD FORBIDS
Kids

HAM AND EGGS
Legs

HORSE AND CART
Heart

HUSBAND AND WIFE
Knife

LION'S LAIR
Chair

MOTHER AND DAUGHTER
Water

PENNY LOCKET
Pocket

RASPBERRY TART
Fart

ROCK OF AGES
Wages

ROLL ME IN THE DIRT
Shirt

SNAKE IN THE GRASS
Looking glass

SUGAR AND HONEY
Money

TIDDLY WINK
Drink

TOTAL WRECK
Check

TROUBLE AND STRIFE
Wife or Life

pad the hoof *v* to walk.
My car broke down, so I had to pad the hoof to work.

plummy *adj* round, jolly, fat.
Dad is so plummy, he's like Santa!

prigger of prauncers *n* a horse thief.

pumblechook *adj* pompous.

punisher *n* an enforcer; a goon.

punk *adj* ill.

rag splawger *n* a rich man.

rasher-wagon *n* frying pan.

red lane *n* the throat.

saucebox *n* mouth.

RED HERRING A red herring is a diversion, or a deliberately misleading clue meant to distract from the actual issue. It's a device often used in mystery writing. The term came about when hunting parties would use hounds to help pursue their quarry. Poachers after the same goal would divert the hounds by creating a scent trail with a pungent fish, thus throwing them off course from the real prey.

sawbones n a doctor.

scraping castle n a restroom.

shine n a disturbance, a row.
I know you're upset, but don't kick up a shine.

sling a slobber v to kiss.

sluicery n a gin shop or public house.

splendiferous adj sumptuous; first-rate.

squeaker n a cross child.
That squeaker in the grocery store was throwing a tantrum in the produce aisle.

star the glaze v to break the window of a shop, take valuable goods, and run away.

swaddy n a soldier.

tallywhags n testicles.

tangle-monger n liar.
She never said a true word—what a tangle-monger.

three-quarter man n an inferior worker.

translated adj extremely drunk.

tumbling down to grass v deteriorating; failing.

vampers n stockings.
I appreciate a nice pair of fishnet vampers.

wattles n ears.

whooper-up n poor singer.

OSCAR WILDE

> "In this world, there are only two tragedies. One is not getting what one wants, and the other is getting it."

He is considered one of the greatest wordsmiths of the 19th century, but Irish dramatist, novelist, and poet Oscar Wilde was far from a proper Victorian gentleman. Born in Dublin in 1854, Oscar attended Magdalene College at Oxford, where he became known for his role in the aesthetic movement. Aesthetes thought that art should convey sensuous pleasure and beauty rather than moral or sentimental messages, and in keeping with this philosophy, Oscar tried his best to make his life a work of art. He was the quintessential dandy who wore his hair long, openly scorned "manly" sports, and decorated his rooms with peacock feathers, flowers, blue china, and other *objets d'art*. At one of his lavish parties, he remarked to friends, "I find it harder and harder every day to live up to my blue china." The line quickly became famous.

He embarked on a lecture tour of North America, where he was slammed by a disapproving press. But Oscar didn't think much of the country anyway, quipping, "America is the only country that went from barbarism to decadence without civilization in between." He eventually settled in London, marrying and having two sons. But perhaps his wife should have been wary of wedding the man who once said, "A man can be happy with any woman as long as he does not love her," for Oscar's desires lay outside of their home. The fact that Oscar idealized youth was evident in his 1891 novel, *The Portrait of Dorian Gray*. That same year, he met an Oxford undergraduate, Alfred Douglas, known as "Bosie," and the two quickly became inseparable. Bosie introduced Oscar to the underworld of gay prostitution, and the older man began keeping company with a number of young working-class male prostitutes. He compared these rendezvous to "feasting with panthers; the danger was half the excitement."

The years of Oscar's friendship with Bosie were some of his most creative. During this time he wrote several plays, including *Lady Windmere's Fan, A Woman of No Importance,* and his most acclaimed, *The Importance of Being Earnest.* But Bosie's father, the Marquess of Queensberry, did not approve of their relationship and accused Oscar of being a "posing sodomite." Wilde, in turn, brought libel charges against Queensberry. After a highly publicized trial, the charges were dropped, and Oscar was left bankrupt. It seemed that, for once, his assertation that, "The only thing worse than being talked about is not being talked about" was not true—the scandal caused many of Oscar's high-society friends to distance themselves from the disgraced writer.

In 1895, Oscar was convicted of gross indecency, which was a felony at the time. He was sentenced to two years' hard labor, which took a great toll on his health. While in prison, he wrote *De Profundis,* a letter to Douglas in which Wilde reflected on his life and spiritual journey. After being released from prison, he spent his last years in exile in France where he composed his last work, *The Ballad of Reading Gaol.* An aesthete to the end, shortly before his death, Oscar was said to remark, "My wallpaper and I are fighting a duel to the death. One of us has got to go." He died in 1900 of cerebral meningitis at the age of forty-six.

He once said, "It is absurd to divide people into good and bad. People are either charming or tedious." And the ever-witty Oscar Wilde could never be called tedious.

"Always forgive your enemies— nothing annoys them so much."

I NEED HIM TO FIX THE SINK, BUT HE'S BUSY *BEATING HIS GUMS* WITH HIS BUDDIES AT THE CLUB!

SHE LOOKED GOOD AT FIRST, BUT WHEN I GOT CLOSER—YIKES! *WHAT A CHUNK OF LEAD!*

Jazz Age Jibes

The Jazz Age was a time of gangsters, gun molls, flappers, bootleggers, and youth gone wild, so it's no wonder that the colorful language of the period was both rich and plentiful. Put on your raccoon coat and boater and try some of these on for size.

all wet *adj* mistaken, misguided, wrong.
If you think I'm going to walk the dog in this thunderstorm, you're all wet.

....

bad face *n* a surly, mean person.

....

balled up *adj* messed up.

....

bearcat *n* a hot-blooded or fiery female.

....

beat one's gums *v* to chatter idly.
I'd like him to help around the house, but he's too busy beating his gums with his buddies down at the club.

....

bee's knees *adj* terrific. Many animal anatomy variations existed, such as elephant's eyebrows, gnat's whistle, eel's hips, caterpillar's kimono, gnat's eyebrows, pig's wings, and snake's hips.

....

blowtop *n* an excitable, violent, or unstable person.
He's such a blowtop that when he died in his video game, he threw the controller against the wall.

....

bug-eyed Betty *n* an unattractive girl.

....

cake-eater *n* a lady's man; a male flirt.

....

catting *v* pursuing women.

....

cheaters *n* eyeglasses or sunglasses.
I can't read that—let me put on my cheaters so I can see better.

....

chin music *n* gossip; idle chatter.

23 SKIDOO! Legend has it that during the Roaring Twenties, young men would gather near New York City's famous Flatiron building on 23rd Street, where the odd shape of the structure created updrafts that would lift women's skirts when they walked past. The leering creeps would be chased off by police officers with a cry of "23 skidoo!" But there are other competing theories as to the origin of this fun-to-say expression.

While the phrase *23 skidoo,* meaning to "go away" or "to leave," became hugely popular in the 1920s, its components are actually somewhat older. "Twenty-three" was once a jocular way of saying "move on" or "get out." How the number 23 became associated with leaving is uncertain, but it may be a reference to Charles Dickens's 1859 novel *A Tale of Two Cities,* wherein the hero, Sydney Carton, is going to the guillotine and is the twenty-third in line. Skidoo is a variant of **skedaddle**, meaning to "depart hurriedly." Regardless of where 23 skidoo came from, if you hear it, you'd best be on your way!

LIQUOR LINGO From 1919 to 1933, Prohibition made the manufacture, sale, and importation of intoxicating liquors illegal in the United States—but **boozehounds** who wanted to imbibe nonetheless found creative ways to get **bent**. **Bootleggers** and **rum runners** brewed noxious spirits and smuggled them throughout the land. A person looking to have a **snort**, or a drink of liquor, could go to a **speakeasy**, a **blind pig**, or a **juice joint**—if he could find one, as these illegal establishments were often kept top secret. At the bar, he might order a glass of good strong **hooch** like **brown plaid** (Scotch whiskey), but if nothing so fine was available, he might have to settle for bootlegged liquor like **bathtub gin** or **white lightning**. A few **belts** of the stuff could get you **blind, hoary-eyed, ossified, splifficated, half under,** or **totally blotto**. If **going on a toot** (a drinking binge) led to **upchuck** (vomit) and a nasty headache, another shot of alcohol, known as **hair of the dog,** could help stave off the misery a little longer. Just hope that last one wasn't poisonous bootleg liquor called **coffin varnish**; though some **ginhounds** might disagree, death is worse than a hangover.

chunk of lead *n* an unattractive female.
She looked good from across the room, but when I got closer—yikes! What a chunk of lead!

....

clinker *n* a mistake; a blunder.

....

collar the jive *v* to be in the know, hip.
I haven't been able to collar the jive since I turned forty.

....

cootie garage *n* hair puffs worn over a woman's ears.

....

crumbcrusher
or **crumbsnatcher** *n* baby or child.
Don't bring your crumbcrusher to the midnight movie.

....

dead soldier *n* an empty bottle.

A DANCE FLOOR MENAGERIE

The names of many jazz dances referred to animals and their movements. See if you can picture what these dance moves looked like:

Bunny Hug
Snake Hips
Camel Walk
Fox-Trot
Fish Tail
Turkey Trot
Cootie Crawl
Grizzly Bear

dewdropper *n* a young man who sleeps all day and doesn't have a job.
That dewdropper's trust fund is so big he'll never have to work.

DOROTHY PARKER

"There's a hell of a difference between wise-cracking and wit. Wit has truth in it; wise-cracking is simply calesthenics with words."

There were few as adept at these verbal calisthenics as American poet, short story writer, critic, and satirist Dorothy Parker. Dorothy began working at *Vogue* in 1914, where she coined snappy captions such as "Brevity is the soul of lingerie." But her career really took off when she was hired as a theater critic for *Vanity Fair* in 1918. In one cutting review of a Broadway performance, she wrote that Katharine Hepburn "runs the gamut of emotions from A to B." Dorothy lunched with her fellow *Vanity Fair* staffers at New York City's Algonquin Hotel every day and became a founding member of the "vicious circle" of writers called The Algonquin Round Table.

Their witty lunchtime repartee was disseminated through members' newspaper columns, and Dorothy was soon known throughout the nation. However, her often stinging reviews offended one producer too many, and she was fired from *Vanity Fair.* She became associated with another venerated periodical in 1925, when the *New Yorker* was founded and she was appointed to the board of editors. In addition to reviews, such as the gem "This is not a novel to be tossed aside lightly. It should be thrown with great force," she contributed many short stories and poems to the magazine. She also published several volumes of verse, two story collections, and a play.

Despite being on top of the literary world, Dorothy had terrible luck in love. She once quipped, "I require three things in a man. He must be handsome, ruthless, and stupid." Perhaps because he didn't meet these qualifications—or perhaps because he did—she divorced her first husband after eleven years of marriage. Dorothy had many short-lived, ill-fated affairs. She married reputedly bisexual actor Alan Campbell in 1934, and the two went to Hollywood to become screenwriters. Though she worked on several successful projects and was nominated for an Academy Award for the screenplay of *A Star Is Born*, Dorothy strongly disliked Hollywood, where, she joked, "the streets are paved with Goldwyn." In the 1930s and '40s, she became active in many political causes and was branded a communist and placed on the Hollywood blacklist. Dorothy's work also suffered because of her alcohol consumption and romantic troubles—she and Campbell divorced and remarried in 1950, and Campbell committed suicide in 1963.

Though her existence was a tempestuous one, Dorothy Parker wouldn't have it any other way. As she once said, "They sicken of the calm, who knew the storm."

"I like to have a martini,
Two at the very most.
After three I'm under the table,
After four I'm under my host!"

dry up *v* shut up, get lost.
Dry up, Dad! I'm going to that party whether you like it or not!

dumb Dora *n* an absolute idiot.

face stretcher *n* an old woman trying to look young.
My mother and a bunch of her face stretcher friends are going to get Botox treatments.

feel a draft *v* to feel something is amiss; to feel hostility directed against oneself.

flat tire *n* a disappointing date.

floorflusher *n* an insatiable dancer.

flour lover *n* a girl with too much face powder.

gazump *v* to swindle.

grummy *adj* depressed.

hamfat *n* an inferior or mediocre entertainer.

handcuff *n* engagement ring.

hawkins *n* a fearsome person.

hayburner *n* a gas-guzzling car or a horse one loses money on.

heavy sugar *n* a lot of money.
He came back from the horse track with some heavy sugar.

heeler *n* a poor dancer.
She's such a heeler she can't even do the Macarena.

HEEBIE JEEBIES AND SCAT SINGING The term "heebie jeebies" is used to describe a feeling of uneasiness, nervousness, or fright. The term can also be used to describe *delirium tremens*, the after-effect of excessive alcohol intake or the intense apprehension that is associated with opiate withdrawal. But in 1926, "Heebie Jeebies" was the title of a hit song recorded by Louis Armstrong and His Hot Five. It includes a famous chorus in which Armstrong does scat singing. **Scat** is a kind of wordless singing, vocal improvisation consisting of gibberish or unintelligible sounds sung to the melody of a standard song.

Legend has it that while recording "Heebie Jeebies," Armstrong's sheet music fell to the ground, so he vocalized a series of nonsense sounds to replace the forgotten lyrics. He expected the cut to be thrown out, but that take of the song was the one released. This story is widely believed to be a myth, but the influence of the recording was nonetheless enormous. Scatting gave jazz singers the ability to improvise with their voices the way musicians could with their instruments.

high hat *n* a snob.
What a high hat that kid is; he won't take public transportation.

....

hinckty *adj* suspicious or snooty, conceited, snobbish.

....

hooey *n* nonsense.

....

iron one's shoelaces: *v* to go to the restroom.

....

jalopy: *n* a dumpy old car.

....

Jeepers Creepers: euphemism for Jesus Christ, used as a mild exclamation of surprise or emotion.

....

jump salty: *v* to become petulant, angry; turn hostile.
That chunk of lead jumped salty when I refused her offer to Camel Walk with her!

know one's onions: *v* to know one's business or what one is talking about.
When it comes to fixing cars, he really knows his onions.

....

licorice stick: *n* clarinet.

....

manacle: *n* wedding ring.

....

parlor-snake: *n* a ladies man.

....

pill-bag: *n* a doctor.
I feel awful; call the pill-bag!

....

pull a Daniel Boone: *v* to vomit.

....

rank: *adj* nasty, disagreeable, stupid.

....

rusty dusty: *n* buttocks.
Get off your rusty dusty and help me carry in the groceries.

scalp doily *n* toupee.
The wind blew his scalp doily askew.

....

smudger *n* a close dancer.

wet blanket: *n* one who prevents others from having a good time.
Don't invite her to the party; she's a real wet blanket.

THE RABBIT DIED The rabbit test was a pregnancy test developed in 1927. Far more complicated (and gruesome) than the tests available today, it consisted of injecting a woman's urine into a female rabbit. Results were not available until a few days later, after examination of the rabbit's ovaries, which would change in a response to a hormone secreted by pregnant women. The rabbit test became widely used and was considered reliable, with an error rate of less than 2%. It was a common misconception that the injected rabbit would die only if the woman was pregnant. Thus, the phrase "the rabbit died" became a euphemism for a positive pregnancy test. In fact, all rabbits used for the test died, because they had to be surgically opened in order to examine the ovaries.

HE MAY LOOK LIKE AN
APPLEHEAD
BUT HE'S THE BEST DARN
CAN OPENER
IN TOWN!

NEVER TAKE A
SHORTIE
WITH A
SHARPIE
OR YOU'LL GET
CHISELED!

Depression-Era Digs

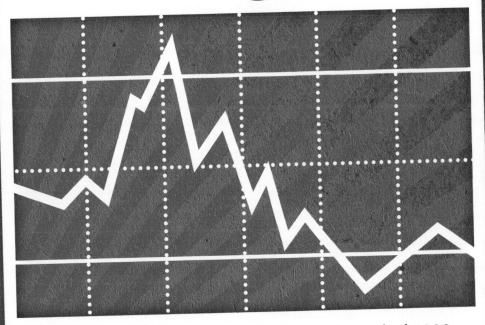

Times were tough for many when the stock market crash of 1929 began a worldwide economic decline. But despite poverty, folks managed to soldier on and even have a gas sometimes— and they coined plenty of clever new sayings along the way.

abdabs *n* the jitters.

above my pay grade a saying meaning "Don't ask me."

ackamarackus *n* nonsense; lies. *They fired the reporter for writing a bunch of ackamarackus.*

active duty *n* a sexually promiscuous male.

acre of corn *n* a prison sentence. *The judge sent him to the big house for an acre of corn.*

alley *n* a drunkard *He's getting to be an alley—without a drink by noon, he gets the abdabs.*

alley apples *n* a pile of horse manure.

amscray *v* Pig Latin for "scram."

antigodlin *adv* diagonally; on a slant.

applehead *n* a stupid person.

armored heifer *n* a can of milk.

bad hat *n* an unscrupulous, dishonest person.

bathtub *n* a motorcycle sidecar.

bevy *n* an alcoholic drink.

big house *n* prison.

bish *n* a mess.

brown-noser *n* an obsequious person, a toady.

bughouse *n* insane asylum.

bull of the woods *n* any important person or authority figure.
I'd better get to work on time, or the bull of the woods will fire me and the security guards will give me the bum's rush.

bum rap *n* an unjust accusation, verdict, or punishment; a false accusation.

bum's rush *n* the ejection of a person from a place by physical force or discourteous treatment.

BUY THE FARM   A person who has "bought the farm" won't be doing any plowing, because he or she is dead. It is thought that this term dates back at least to World War II, when each member of the U.S. armed services was issued a life insurance policy in the amount of $10,000, a great deal of money in those days. Many of the troops were unmarried young men who named their parents as beneficiaries, and many of the parents lived on farms. If their son was killed, his insurance would be used to pay off the mortgage on the farm.

DASHIELL HAMMETT

The "dean of the . . . 'hard-boiled' school of detective fiction," according to his obituary in the *New York Times,* Dashiell Hammett was perhaps the most influential American writer of the genre, creator of the legendary private eye Sam Spade. After working as a detective himself, Hammett became a writer, publishing five novels between 1929 and his death in 1961, including *The Maltese Falcon* and *The Thin Man.* His oft-quoted tough-guy Sam Spade remains enormously popular today, as well as his characters Nick and Nora Charles, the sophisticated couple who solved mysteries while exchanging clever repartee.

"Who shot him?" I asked. The grey man scratched the back of his neck and said, "Somebody with a gun."
—*RED HARVEST*

"The cheaper the crook, the gaudier the patter."
—*THE MALTESE FALCON*

"A cunning gleam came into his one open eye as he looked at the lighter. The gleam was not sane."
—*THE GLASS KEY*

"The problem with putting two and two together is that sometimes you get four, and sometimes you get twenty-two."
— *THE THIN MAN*

"Listen, Dundy, it's been a long time since I burst into tears because a policeman didn't like me."
—*THE MALTESE FALCON*

"Money's good stuff. I haven't anything against it."
—*THE BIG KNOCKOVER*

"She grinned at me. 'You got types?'
'Only you, darling—lanky brunettes with wicked jaws.'"
— *THE THIN MAN*

"The face she made at me was probably meant for a smile. Whatever it was, it beat me. I was afraid she'd do it again, so I surrendered."
—*THE CONTINENTAL OP*

"I haven't lived a good life. I've been bad, worse than you could know."
"You know, that's good, because if you actually were as innocent as you pretend to be, we'd never get anywhere."
—*THE MALTESE FALCON*

"How do you feel?" "Terrible. I must've gone to bed sober."
— *THE THIN MAN*

bumpman *n* a pickpocket.

business, the *n* rough treatment; a beating or murder.
A gang of kids broke into the store and gave the clerk the business before robbing the place.

bust a gut *v* to use all one's strength to accomplish a task; to try so hard one risks injury.

can opener *n* safe-cracker.

cheek it *v* to bluff.
If you don't know the answer, just cheek it!

chew out *v* to reprimand.
The policeman chewed out the bumpman and the can-opener for breaking the law.

Chicago typewriter *n* a submachine gun.
The gangsters mowed down the rival gang with their Chicago typewriters.

chisel *v* to cheat.

chrome-dome *n* a bald-headed man.

clock-watcher *n* a person who takes little interest in work; someone who watches the clock until quitting time.

collar a nod *v* to sleep.
Hopefully I'll have time to collar a nod on the flight.

cook with gas *v* to do something right.

GOING POSTAL During World War II, the military was careful to keep information that could be used by the enemy from getting into the wrong hands. The slogan "Loose lips sink ships" was used to remind people not to reveal sensitive information such as troop locations. To maintain some privacy, many writers began to use colorful acronyms in their letters:

SWALK
Sealed With A Loving Kiss

HOLLAND
*Hope Our Love Lives
(or Lasts) And Never Dies*

ITALY
*I Trust And Love You or
I'm Thinking About Loving You*

FRANCE
*Friendship Remains
And Never Can End*

BURMA
*Be Undressed (or Upstairs)
Ready My Angel*

MALAYA
*My Ardent Lips
Await Your Arrival*

NORWICH
*(k)Nickers Off Ready
When I Come Home*

BOLTOP
*Better On Lips
Than On Paper*

CHINA
*Come Home I'm
Naked Already*

JAPAN
Just A Piece A Night

RAYMOND CHANDLER

Fortunately for fans of hard-boiled detective stories, the Depression (and, apparently, his fondness for strong drink) cost Raymond Chandler his job as an oil company executive, and the then 44-year-old decided to take up a new career as a writer. Between 1939 and 1959, Chandler published seven novels featuring the tough-talking private eye Philip Marlowe. The title of Chandler's first detective novel, *The Big Sleep,* immediately joined the lexicon as a synonym for death. Marlowe, with his distinctive style, remains synonymous with the hard-boiled detective today.

"The streets were dark with something more than night."
—*TROUBLE IS MY BUSINESS*

"You're broke, eh?"
"I been shaking two nickels together for a month, trying to get them to mate."
—*THE BIG SLEEP*

"To say she had a face that would have stopped a clock would have been to insult her. It would have stopped a runaway horse."
—*THE LITTLE SISTER*

"Alcohol is like love," he said. "The first kiss is magic, the second is intimate, the third is routine. After that you take the girl's clothes off."
—*THE LONG GOODBYE*

"I'm all done with hating you. It's all washed out of me. I hate people hard, but I don't hate them very long."
—*THE LADY IN THE LAKE*

"I like smooth, shiny girls, hardboiled and loaded with sin."
—*FAREWELL, MY LOVELY*

"As honest as you can expect a man to be in a world where it's going out of style."
—*THE BIG SLEEP*

"From 30 feet away she looked like a lot of class. From 10 feet away she looked like something made up to be seen from 30 feet away. "
—*THE HIGH WINDOW*

cookie pusher *n* someone who does little work and tries to get ahead by kissing up to the boss.
Why don't you do some work instead of being such a cookie pusher?

cowboy coffee *n* black coffee without sugar.

crocked *adj* drunk.

cross palms *v* to bribe.
The bad hat club owner regularly crossed palms with the cops to stay out of the Big House.

cutting out [paper] dolls *adj* crazy.

dead hoofer *n* a poor dancer.

deck *n* a pack of cigarettes.

diddly-squat *n* not much; a small amount.

dilly *n* a person or thing remarkable in size, quality, or appearance.

ding bat *n* a silly person.

doggo *adj* in hiding; wanting to be left alone.
After showing himself to be such a dead hoofer on the dance floor, he was so embarassed that he went doggo.

dogs *n* feet.
After standing in line for concert tickets, my dogs were barking.

doll dizzy *adj* crazy about women, devoted to skirt-chasing

dough *n* money.

drugstore cowboy *n* a young man who hangs around public places trying to show off and impress the opposite sex.

ducky shincracker *n* a good dancer.
That ducky shincracker is burning up the dance floor.

eager beaver *n* an enthusiastic helper.

eye-opener *n* an early morning drink of alcohol.

eyewash *n* nonsense.

fakeloo artist *n* con artist.
The fakeloo artist targets fat-heads and feebs.

fat-head *n* a dense or foolish person.

feather-legs *n* a deceitful person.
You can't trust that feather-legs girlfriend of yours to go on spring break without you.

feeb *n* a feeble-minded person; an imbecile.

flip your wig *v* to lose control of yourself.

foo-foo dust *n* a narcotic in powdered form.

frail eel *n* a pretty girl.
He flipped his wig over that frail eel.

fuddy-duddy *n* an old-fashioned person.

fuzz *n* the police.
Amscray! It's the fuzz!

SOLDIER SLANG In many countries, World War II marked the end of the Depression. There were new jobs available on the homefront making munitions and supplies, and, of course, soldiers were needed on the front lines. Here are some military slang terms that they might have used.

ACK-ACK
Anti-aircraft fire

BAT ONE'S GUMS
To talk idly but loudly

BATTERY ACID
Coffee

BLANKET DRILL
A nap or sleep

BRASS-POUNDER
A telegraph operator

BUZZARD COLONEL
A full colonel in the U.S. Army

CHINA CLIPPER
A dishwasher

CITY COW
Canned milk

COVERED WAGON
An aircraft carrier

DAY THE EAGLE SCREAMS
Pay day

DOODLEBUG
The German V-1 flying bomb

EGGBEATER
An airplane propeller

FIFTH COLUMN
Covert activities or sabotage

FLUB THE DUB
To evade one's duty; to loaf

FLYBOY
Aviator, member of the airborne service

GEDUNK
Ice cream, candy or any dessert

GRAVEL AGITATOR
An infantryman

HICKBOO
An enemy air raid

JUNGLE JUICE
Illegal, home-brewed liquor

KILROY WAS HERE
Popular wartime American graffiti slogan

LATRINE RUMOR
An unsubstantiated, often exaggerated story or rumor

MAE WEST
A type of inflatable life jacket that resembles a bosom

OVERCOAT
Parachute

POOP SHEET
Work detail listing

PRESQUAWK
To inspect a piece of work before an official inspection

ROCK-SLINGER
A mortar operator

ROLL UP ONE'S FLAPS
To stop talking

SACK RAT
One who spends most free time napping

SIN-HOUND
A chaplain

gas *n* a good time, or something really funny.

gasper *n* cigarette.
The condemned man requested one last gasper.

gaunch *n* an unpopular girl.

gazoozle *v* to cheat.
You gazoozled at cards!

giggle-juice *n* booze.

gobbledygook *n* double talk; long, nonsensical speech.
I tried to listen to his budget proposal, but it sounded like a bunch of gobbledygook.

grandstand *v* to show off.

greed-up *adj* high on opium.

gripes my cookies *v* to make extremely annoyed; to irritate.

gumshoe *n* detective.

harp-polisher *n* a clergyman, especially a priest.

hen fruit *n* eggs.

hep-cat *n* a performer or fan of swing and jazz music.

hi-de-ho *exc* hello.

hot squat *n* the electric chair.

house dick *n* a detective employed by a hotel.

hugger-mugger *adj* slovenly; makeshift; or secret, clandestine.

in cahoots *adj* conspiring with.
The gumshoe figured out that the house dick was in cahoots with the cat burglars.

jiggery pokery *n* trickery.

jingle-brained *adj* not very intelligent; confused.

juiced *adj* drunk.

keister *n* buttocks.

khaki wacky *adj* boy crazy.

killer-diller *n* an excellent thing or person.
My new car is just killer-diller.

kittle-cattle *n* an unreliable person or group of people.

lettuce *n* money.

little shaver *n* a young boy.

Mary Warner *n* marajuana.

meat wagon *n* ambulance.

moldy fig *n* a prude; one whose views or tastes are old fashioned.

moll *n* a gangster's girlfriend.

motorized freckles *n* insects.

mug *n* face.

mug-up *n* a snack.

office-copy *n* a second drink.

Okie *n* during the Dust-bowl years, a very poor migrant in search of work.

TRAVELER TALK

During the Great Depression, thousands of men and even some women became hoboes, traveling the roads and railways in search of work. Here is some of the colorful language you might have heard on the road.

ACE NOTE
A one-dollar bill

ALL TRAMPS SENT FREE
Atchinson, Topeka & Santa Fe Railroad

AXLE-GREASE
Butter

BATTLESHIP
A steel-sided coal car

BEEFER
Complainer

BONE POLISHER
A nasty dog

CANNONBALL
A fast train

CARRY THE BANNER
Walk all night without finding shelter

COLD, HUNGRY AND DAMP
Cincinnati, Hamilton & Dayton Railroad

CRIMPS
Rheumatism

DECORATE THE MAHOGANY
Buy a round of drinks

DITCH
To throw off the train

FREEZER
Refrigerator car

GANDY DANCER
Railroad worker who laid track

GOOSEBERRY BUSH
Clothesline

GREASE THE TRACK
Get run over by a train

HIT GROUNDERS
Collect cigarette butts

LESS SLEEP AND MORE SPEED
Lake Shore & Michigan Southern Railroad

NICKEL FLOP
A 24-hour (or open-all-night) movie house

NICKEL NOTE
Five-dollar bill

ODD FELLOWS
Three donuts and a cup of coffee

POLISH THE MUG
To clean one's face

RED BALL
Fast train

REMITTANCE MAN
A hobo paid by his family to stay on the road

SHEETS
Newspapers to sleep on

SHIRT RABBITS
Body lice

SNAPPER RIG
Secondhand clothing

TAKE YOUR PARCELS AND WALK
Texas Pacific & Western Railroad

YEGG
A thief

P.D.Q. *adj* pretty damn quick.

pass the buck *v* to pass responsibility to another.

pennies from heaven *n* easy money.
We won the lottery—it's pennies from heaven!

piece of trade *n* a prostitute; a promiscuous woman.

plonk *n* cheap wine.

porchclimber *n* moonshine.

pour on the cool *v* drive fast.

rationed *adj* in a relationship.
Hi, sugar, are you rationed?

rhubarb *n* a noisy argument, especially on a baseball field.

ringy *adj* angry.

rumpy *adj* excellent.

schmendrik *n* foolish person.

sensay *adj* sensational.

seven out *v* lose a bet.

shamus *n* a detective.

share crop *n* a sexually promiscuous female.

sharpie *n* swindler.

shortie *n* a small drink of alcohol.
Never take a shortie with a sharpie or you'll get chiseled.

skid row *n* an area of town frequented by vagrants.

snap your cap *v* to get angry.

snurge *n* an unlikeable person.

spondulicks *n* money.

stemwinder *n* an aggressive talker.

stewed to the gills *n* extremely drunk.

stocious *adj* drunk.

stompers *n* shoes.

stumblebum *n* a lazy person.

take a powder *v* to leave.

tatty *adj* in poor condition; shabby.

tear it up *v* to perform with excitement.

troppo *adj* mentally unhinged.

up-and-downer *n* a violent argument.

what's buzzin', cousin? "How's it going?"

whinge *v* to complain incessantly. *She can't come over to my place because she's always whinging about how she's allergic to my cats.*

whizzer *n* pickpocket.

woofits *n* depression.

worb *n* a slovenly person.

yob *n* a violent person; a thug.

WHEN I HEARD THE DOG WALKER LOST MY NEW PUPPY AT THE PARK, I ABSOLUTELY ***WENT APE!!***

SHE ORDERED THE ***CLUCK-AND-GRUNT*** WITH A ***BURNT BRITISH.***

Cold War Cuts

A forty-year standoff between the Western world and Communist powers inspired some fighting words. But the 1950s, '60s and '70s also saw social changes as postwar prosperity led to the Age of Aquarius with plenty of good vibes. Can you dig it?

A-bomb *n* an exceptionally fast car; a hot rod.

backatcha *exc* "you, too"; usually a response to a compliment.
"You look marvelous!" "Backatcha!"

badger gassing *v* breaking wind.

baloney *n* nonsense.

bam! *exc* used to express satisfaction at accomplishing something.

Bamboo Curtain *n* the Communist states of Asia during the Cold War.

bangin' *adj* attractive, exciting.

beatnik *n* a nonconformist; member of the Beat Generation.

behind the Iron Curtain *adj* in the Soviet Union.

Big Brother *n* authority figure; the government.
Don't do anything you wouldn't want Big Brother to see!

bitchin' *adj* awesome, good, great.

blazin' *v* smoking marijuana.

blitzed *adj* drunk.

bogue *adj* short for bogus; offensive or unrealistic.

boho *n* bohemian; an artistic type.

bohunk *n* a derogatory term for a Slavic immigrant.

BIKINI Radioactive was once slang for "very popular," and nothing boosts a girl's popularity like wearing a skimpy swimsuit. Perhaps that's why the bikini is named for a nuclear weapons test site. In the summer of 1946, Jacques Heim, a French designer from Cannes, debuted a revealing two-piece swimsuit dubbed the *atome* (French for "atom"). He promoted it as "The world's smallest bathing suit." But just three weeks later, Louis Réard—an engineer turned designer who was running his mother's shoe shop in Paris—introduced a swimsuit that was even smaller. Made out of just 30 inches of fabric, Reard's creation was basically a bra top and two inverted triangles of cloth connected with string. He called it a bikini, after the Bikini Atoll island in the South Pacific, a place in the news at that time since the United States conducted the first post-war test of an atomic weapon there just days before the debut of the risqué new swimsuit. Although two-piece bathing suits had been in existence before the bikini, none of them were quite as revealing or as popular as this new invention, which dared to expose even the wearer's navel. In one ad campaign, Réard declared that a two-piece wasn't a real bikini "unless it could be pulled through a wedding ring."

THE COUNTER CULTURE

During the 1960s and early 1970s, young people around the world began to reject the rigid social rules and expectations that they associated with their parents' generation, and embraced a freer lifestyle that promoted equality, experimentation, and peace. These youths loosely embraced many different kinds of social activism, including the antiwar movement, the civil rights movement, the women's movement, environmentalism, Eastern spirituality, and the sexual revolution. If you were a college student in this era, you might have been inspired to reject mainstream pressures to conform and instead *drop out* and *do whatever turns you on.* If you decided to experiment with drugs, you might visit a *head shop* to buy some *roach clips.* You could have a *mind-blowing experience* by *getting stoned* on *weed* or *grass* (especially if you could get *Acapulco Gold* or *Maui Wowie*), which would make you feel *mellow* but later might give you *the munchies.* If you got hold of a *blotter* of *acid,* which could have been *purple haze* or *orange sunshine,* you might find yourself *tripping.* With luck, you wouldn't have a *bad trip* or experience *flashbacks* later.

If someone invited you to a *happening* or a *be-in,* you might reply enthusiastically by saying *"Far out!"* or *"Outta sight!"* A great party at a friend's *pad* would be *where it's at,* a totally funky *scene,* full of *foxy chicks* and *groovy* guys wearing *great threads* such as *bell bottoms* or *hip huggers, dashikis, granny glasses,* and *love beads.* Later, you might attend a rally, where you would chant *"Make love, not war!"* and *"Hell, no, we won't go"* or *"Power to the people!"* Everyone would flash peace signs by making a "V" with two fingers, and they'd ask passersby, *"Can you dig it?"* If they could, they'd reply, *"Right on, man."* If some *uptight squares* thought you were experiencing *reefer madness,* they might call the *pigs* to come and arrest you. Chagrined, you might decide to *sell out* and join the establishment, working for *the man.* Or maybe you would *stay cool* and *turn on, tune in, and drop out.*

boob tube *n* televison.
Anything good on the boob tube?

....

bootin' *v* roller-skating while dancing.
We can't decide wether to go boogie at a disco or bootin' at the rink.

....

boss *adj* excellent, superior.

....

bread *n* money; cash.

....

brinkmanship *n* Cold War policy of using nuclear intimidation.

....

buds *n* marijuana.

....

bugging out *v* overreacting; showing panic, alarm, or paranoia.
My dad's bugging out because I got a bad grade in math.

....

bummer *n* bad news.

burlap *n* loss of a job due to firing.
After getting drunk at a client lunch, I was given the burlap.

....

burn *v* to disrespect, embarrass, or insult someone.

....

busted *v* to get caught doing something you shouldn't be doing.

....

buzz off *exc* meaning "go away!"

....

catch one's drift *v* to understand.

....

Check-point Charlie *n* Berlin Wall crossing point.

....

cheese-eater *n* an informer; a person who betrays, denies, or abandons his or her associates, social group, or beliefs.
That cheese-eater sold us out to Big Brother!

cheesy *adj* shabby, cheap.

china *n* teeth.
He looks great since he got his braces off his china.

choice *adj* of high quality.

chump *n* a fool; a loser.

clink *n* prison.

cool it *v* stop.

copacetic *adj* very satisfactory; excellent.
I love your crib, it's copacetic!

crib *n* one's home.

FLOWER CHILD In the 1960s, San Francisco's Haight-Ashbury district was ground zero for hippie culture. The first "flower children" there were neighborhood kids who made and sold paper flowers to tourists. Eventually, the flower child moniker became synonymous with the idealistic young people who gathered in San Francisco in 1967's Summer of Love. Flower children wore flowers in their hair and distributed flowers to symbolize ideals of brotherhood, peace, and love. These ideals and actions became known as **flower power.**

crucial *adj* great, very cool.

Deadhead *n* a diehard fan of the Grateful Dead.

deece *adj* abbreviation of decent; not too bad.
I can't say the sequel to that movie was as good as the original, but it was deece.

dig *v* to understand.
Can you dig it?

disco biscuits *n* Quaaludes.

Domino Theory *n* Cold War belief that if a country comes under communist control, neighboring nations will follow.

don't have a cow *exc* calm down.
Don't have a cow. Just do what we learned in the duck-and-cover drills.

doobie or doobage *n* a marijuana cigarette.

doofus *n* a foolish, incompetent, or stupid person.

dork *n* a slow-witted person; one who is socially inept or out of touch with contemporary trends.

drag *n* someone or something that is depressing.

duck-and-cover *v* to lie facedown and protect one's skin in the event of a sudden nuclear attack.

dynamite *adj* excellent.

fab *adj* short for fabulous.

fall-out shelter *n* an underground structure that provides shelter from a nuclear attack.

far out *adj* great, unconventional, extraordinary.

fight a bottle *v* to drink alcohol from a bottle.

fire stick *n* a gun.

flapjaw *n* talk; chat.

flub-dub *n* awkwardness; ineptitude.
If it weren't for his flub-dub, we'd be inside that club right now.

four-on-the-floor *n* four-speed manual transmission with floor-mounted gearbox.

freaky-deaky *adj* very weird.

funkadelic *adj* absolutely amazing; the funkiest.

funky *adj* stylish and hip.

gas *n* something that is fantastic, thrilling, or delightful.
That party was fantastic! What a gas!

gearhead *n* a person who is extremely interested and knowledgeable about cars.

gee whiz *exc* an expression of surprise, dismay, or enthusiasm.

geek *n* a person regarded as unattractive, socially awkward, and overly intellectual.

get bent *v* to get drunk or high on drugs.

gig *n* a concert, or a job.

go ape *v* to become enraged. *When I heard that the dog walker had lost my new puppy at the park, I absolutely went ape.*

go bananas *v* to go crazy, get extremely excited.

good vibes *n* positive energy. *The yoga studio has good vibes.*

goon *n* a hired hoodlum or thug; or an ugly or stupid person.

graum *v* to annoy; to worry.

gravy *n* something extra; gain acquired with little effort, especially above that needed for ordinary living. *She hoped the bake sale would earn enough to cover the cost of the school trip; anything more would be gravy.*

groovy *adj* marvelous, wonderful, excellent.

hairy eyeball *n* a look of disapproval. *The teacher gave me the hairy eyeball when I tried to pass a note.*

hang *v* to spend time or exist with a person or in a space.

head *n* a regular user of drugs.

LESS TALK, MORE ROCK It emerged in the 1950s as the sound of teenage rebellion, and today rock music has a staggering number of subgenres. Here are just a few of the types of rock 'n' roll that developed.

ROCKABILLY
One of the earliest styles of rock-and-roll music played in the mid-1950s by white singers such as Elvis Presley, Carl Perkins, and Jerry Lee Lewis.

DOO WOP
One of the most popular forms of rock and roll in the 1950s and 1960s, featuring multi-part vocal harmonies and nonsense backing lyrics.

SKIFFLE
Features jazz, blues, and folk influences, usually using homemade or improvised instruments such as the washboard, jugs, tea chest bass, cigar-box fiddle, and musical saw.

MERSEYBEAT
Refers to bands from Liverpool, England, on the River Mersey with simple guitar-dominated lineups and catchy tunes.

BLUES ROCK
Characterized by bluesy improvisation and extended electric-guitar jams.

FOLK ROCK
Combines traditional folk music and rock and features clear vocal harmonies and jangly guitar sounds.

PSYCHEDELIC ROCK
Attempts to replicate the effects and enhance the mind-altering experiences of hallucinogenic drugs.

heavy *adj* serious or important.

hefty *n* a heavy man.

hippie *n* a usually young person who rejects the mores of established society and advocates a non-conformist, nonviolent ethic; a long-haired, unconventionally dressed young person.

hood *n* a hoodlum; rowdy or violent young person.
My grandmother can't tell the difference between hippies and hoods.

hotdog! an exclamation of delight.

hot-dogger *n* show-off.

house larry *n* a man who frequents a retail store without buying.

hubba hubba exclamation used when observing an attractive person.

hunk *n* an attractive male.
Hubba hubba! That guy's a hunk!

hunky-dory *adj* great.

in a swivet *adj* hurried, anxious, fidgety.

in-and-outer *n* a mediocre performer or athlete.

jacker-upper *n* one who raises the price on something.

jinkies *exc* an expression of surprise.

jive turkey *n* a person who is unreliable, makes empty promises, or is full of bluster.

jonesing *v* craving; desperate for something.

joshing *v* kidding, joking around.

juice bar *n* a bar that served only non-alcoholic drinks that catered to people who liked to dance.

jump one's bones *v* to have sexual intercourse.

keen *adj* having or showing eagerness or enthusiasm.

keeping it real *v* being true to yourself and your values; not being phony.
My friends keep trying to convince me to run a 10K race with them, but I'm keeping it real and sticking to my exercise program of reaching for the TV remote.

kicks *n* running shoes.

killer *adj* excellent, or very difficult.

klupper *n* a slow worker; a slow-moving, slow-talking, slow-thinking person.

knothead *n* an incompetent or stupid person.

lay a gasser *v* to fart.
The person next to me on the bus laid a gasser and everyone seemed to think it was me.

mackin' *v* flirting or trying to pick up women.

man, the *n* the establishment; an authority figure or entity such as the government, corporations, or law enforcement.

mint *adj* perfect, in good condition.

mole *n* double agent; undercover agent.

moolah *n* money, cash.

Mutual Assured Destruction

n Cold War military strategy in which a buildup of nuclear weapons was believed to prevent either side from launching a first strike.

narc *n* abbreviation for narcotics officer; snitch or tattletale.

neato *adj* neat, great.

nifty *adj* very good or effective.

old lady *n* girlfriend or wife.

old man *n* n boyfriend or husband.

outta sight *adj* very good, enjoyable.
Your pad is groovy; it's outta sight!

pad *n* a home, especially an apartment.

papoose *n* a nonunion worker working with union workers.

passion pit *n* drive-in movie theater.
We saw a flick at the passion pit.

penman *n* a forger; a student who signs his parent's signature on school correspondence.

plastic *adj* fake, phony, not real.

poindexter *n* a nerdy intellectual.

pop a wheelie *v* to lift the front wheel while riding a bike.

LUNCH-COUNTER LINGO

The diner: It's the classic mid-century meeting place. Linger over a cup of hot coffee and a piece of pie served by a friendly hash-slinger who calls you "Sweetie," play a few tunes on the jukebox, and soon life seems a little bit better. They call it comfort food for a reason. If you've spent a lot of time at diners, lunch counters, or greasy spoons, you may have heard some of the slang used by waitstaff and cooks. There's evidence that this lingo may have been used by waiters as early as the 1870s, and it was popular up until the 1970s. Since computers are now widely used in the ordering process, there is no longer as much need for these helpful mnemonic devices.

ADAM AND EVE ON A RAFT
Two poached eggs on toast

ADAM'S ALE
Water

BIRDSEED
Breakfast cereal

BOW-WOW
Hot dog

BRONX VANILLA
Garlic

BUBBLE DANCER
Dishwasher

BURN THE BRITISH
Toasted English muffin

BUTCHER'S REVENGE
Meatloaf

CLUCK AND GRUNT
Eggs and bacon

COW FEED
Salad

COW PASTE
Butter

DIRTY WATER
Coffee

FIRST LADY
An order of ribs

FROG STICKS
French fries

HOCKEY PUCK
Well-done hamburger

HOLD THE GRASS
No lettuce

MOTOR OIL
Syrup

NERVOUS PUDDING
Bowl of Jell-O

NOAH'S BOY
Slice of ham

SOUP JOCKEY
Waitress

TWO DOTS AND A DASH
Two fried eggs and a strip of bacon

WALK A COW THROUGH THE GARDEN
Burger with lettuce, tomato, and onion

WHISTLE BERRIES
Baked beans

YELLOW PAINT
Mustard

YUM-YUM
Sugar

preppy *n* a student at or a graduate of a preparatory school, or someone who dresses like one.

primo *adj* high quality, excellent, the best.

pruneface *n* a homely or sad-looking person.

psyched *adj* excited, energized.

rah *n* a cheerleader.

ralph *v* to vomit.
Ugh; she got carsick and ralphed.

ream out *v* to scold someone severely.

Red *adj* Communist.
Just because he's dating a Russkie, they accuse him of being a Red.

refusenik *n* a would-be emigrant denied permission to leave the Soviet Union.

right on an expression of agreement, affirmation.

righteous *adj* excellent, genuine.

Russkie *n* Russian.

scumbag *n* a disgusting, disreputable, low-life person.

seppo *adj* one who has legally separated from his or her spouse.
He's out on the prowl again now that he and his wife are seppo.

shaggin' wagon *n* a customized van with a bed in it; any vehicle used as a place to have sexual intercourse.

RED SCARE In 1950, Senator Joseph McCarthy claimed to have a list of known Communists working for the U.S. State Department and spearheaded hearings to expose Soviet sympathizers. The reputations that were damaged in this witch hunt far outnumbered the agents of espionage uncovered. Making accusations of disloyalty, subversion, or treason without evidence is now known as **McCarthyism**.

The director of the FBI during this period, the infamous J. Edgar Hoover, wrote in his 1958 book *Masters of Deceit* that there were five types of Communists of whom patriotic Americans should beware. The worst was the **card-carrying Communist,** who openly belonged to the party; next was the **underground Communist,** who was secretly a member of the party; third was the **Communist sympathizer,** someone who believed in the Communists' goals; fourth was the **fellow traveler,** who agreed with some of the Communist views; and finally, the **dupe,** which could be anyone whose opinions might be helpful to Communists, such as a pacifist.

These are some popular slang terms for Communists during the Red Scare.

BOLSHEVIK	**LEFTY**
COMMIE	**PINKO**
COMRADE	**PINKERTON**

SURFER SLANG Though surfing originated with the early Polynesians, it was in 1950s California that it began to gain the worldwide popularity it now holds. Movies like *Gidget* and musicians like the Beach Boys brought the sun-and-surf ethos to the world. Surf culture developed its own lingo, which is full of lively expressions based on the waves, weather, location, and crowd.

ATE IT
Wiped out

BAGGIES
Surf shorts

BANZAI PIPELINE
Legendary Oahu break

BARREL
Hollow part of the wave; the tube.

BOGUS
Wrong; offensive

COMB
The crest of a wave

COWABUNGA
Exclamation of joy or excitement

CRUM BUM
Bad wave

CURL
The inside top of a wave, where it curves as it breaks

GOOFY FOOT
A person who surfs with the right leg forward

HANG TEN
Surfing move with ten toes over the edge of the board

HANGIN' LOOSE
Relaxed but in control

HAOLE
Greeting, originally Hawaiian

LOCALS
Crew who regularly surf the same spot

POCKET
Steepest, fastest part of a wave, right in front of where it breaks

RIPPER
Shredder

SHOOT THE CURL
When a surfer rides along the breaking part of the wave

SHREDDER
A fantastic surfer

STOKED
Very excited

THONGS
Flip-flops

THRASHED
Pounded by a wave

TUBE
The crest of a wave that curls around a surfer; the barrel

WAHINE
Female surfer

WAVEHOG
One who takes all the best waves

WOODY
Faux-wood paneled station wagon, good for toting surfboards

sick *adj* very good, excellent, awesome.

....

sit-upon *n* the buttocks.

....

ski-bunny *n* a female skier who is more interested in being seen on the slopes than skiing.

....

skinny *n* the real deal or truth.

slammin' *adj* awesome.

....

something else *adj* great, excellent.

....

spheroid *n* a baseball.

....

spizzerinktum *n* vigor, pep.
I need coffee in the morning to give me some spizzerinktum.

VIETNAM WAR The Vietnam War was fought between the Communist state of North Vietnam and South Vietnam, aided by the United States. As with any war, in terms of slang, the Vietnam War yielded a lot of unique terminology, much of which was absorbed into popular culture.

BOONIES
Far out in the field

CHOP CHOP
Food

DIDI MAU
To leave

FUBAR
Fouled up beyond all recognition

GRUNT
An infrantryman or foot soldier

IN-COUNTRY
In Vietnam

square *n* a boring, un-hip person.

....

step off *v* back off.

....

stone fox *n* a very attractive, sexy person.

....

streak *v* to run in public in the nude. *Someone streaked across the field at the football game!*

....

stud *n* a promiscuous male.

....

that's the way the ball bounces *exp* that's life.

....

to the bone *adj* totally; completely.

....

to the max *n* the maximum; the most it can be.

....

toking up *v* the act of smoking marijuana.

tomato *n* a very attractive young woman.

....

trippendicular *adj* totally amazing, fantastic.

....

trippy *adj* of, relating to, or suggestive of a trip on psychedelic drugs or the culture associated with such drugs.

....

tubular *adj* awesome, excellent, very good.

....

tuff *adj* cool or sharp in a rugged way.

....

wastoid a drug user.

....

wazoo *n* a person's rear end.

....

wig out *v* to panic, lose control; get excited about something.

OH, THAT DWEEB HAS A THING FOR ME? GAG ME WITH A SPOON!
STOP HARSHING MY MELLOW!

Pop Culture Phrases

In the millennial years, as the 20th century gave way to the 21st, pop culture became paramount and digital media exploded, expanding communication in all sorts of new ways—and bringing new slang with it.

all day and a night *n* a life sentence without parole.
After his third strike, the judge gave him all day and a night.

....

amped *adj* excited about something.
I am so amped about riding that new quadruple-loop roller coaster, bro!

....

bad-ass *adj* very good, awesome; skilled.

....

bee-yatch *n* rude variation on "bitch."

....

bimbo *n* an attractive but vacuous person.

....

bite me *exc* meaning "I don't care" or "bug off!"

bling *n* gaudy, flashy, or expensive jewelry worn to show off wealth.

....

blood *n* member of a street gang; a friend.
Wassup, blood?

....

blow off *v* to skip, avoid, or ignore someone or something.

....

bomb, the *n* something favorable; excellent.

....

bomb diggity *n* something great or fabulous.
That new restaurant is the bomb diggity!

....

boo-yah an expression of triumph; "Take that!"

....

booty *n* buttocks.

boy toy *n* boyfriend.

brutal *adj* the worst.

buff *adj* physically well built; in good shape.

burn-out *n* a regular user of drugs; one whose wits have been dulled from smoking too much.

cha-ching *adj* expensive, extremely costly.

chocoholic *n* someone addicted to chocolate.
Without her fix every day, she goes into a chocoholic rage.

cold lampin' *v* posturing.

craptacular *adj* spectacularly awful.

digits *n* a phone number.

dirtbag *n* a person who is utterly foul, both morally and hygienically.
Ugh, no way is that dirtbag getting in my car!

ditzy *adj* silly; foolish.

do me a solid *v* do me a favor.
You're going to the grocery store? Do me a solid and pick up some cereal while you're there.

don't go there! phrase meaning "I don't wan't to talk about it."

dope *adj* extremely cool.

down with *adj* in agreement about something.
I'm totally down with you on the need for more vacation time.

HIP HOP HISTORY

Hip-hop culture emerged in the 1970s in New York's South Bronx, where innovative DJs and MCs, battling breakdance crews, and bold graffiti artists came together to create a new sound and style. It quickly spread beyond the block to urban communities across the United States, and today hip-hop is a global phenomenon.

AW-ITE
All right

B-BOY
Breakdancer

BEATBOXING
Vocal percussion, using just the mouth to create beats

BEATS
Rhythms

BITER
Copier

BOO
Boyfriend or girlfriend

BUGGIN'
Acting strange; freaking out

CHILLIN'
Relaxing

DEAD PRESIDENTS
Paper money

DEF
Cool; great

DIS
To show disrespect

FITTY
Fifty

FLOW
Rap

FLY
Attractive, sexy

FRESH
New and great

FRONT
To fake or pretend

GANGSTA
Gang-related

HOMIE
Friend or pal (also homeboy, homeslice, homeskillet)

ILL
Cool; good

ON THE GRIND
Selling drugs; making money on the street

PEEPS
Friends

PHAT
Attractive; cool

PLAYA
A guy with a lot of girlfriends

SHORTY
Girl or girlfriend

WACK
Bad

WHAT'S THE DILLY, YO?
What's going on?

WORD; WORD UP
An affirmation; agreement

eat my shorts *exc* go to hell.

fart-knocker *n* idiot; jerk.

fly *adj* cool; fun.

freak out *v* to panic, lose control.
My dad would totally freak out if he found out about me joyriding in his convertible.

fronting *v* pretending to be something you're not.

get down *v* to dance.

gnarly *adj* distasteful, distressing, offensive; or awesome, great.

grill *n* teeth, dental work; one's personal space.
Don't get all up in my grill, man—step off!

harsh one's mellow *v* to upset or annoy someone.
Yes, I know tomorrow is Monday and we've got to go back to work, but can you stop talking about it? It's harshing my mellow.

heinous *adj* awful, the worst.

hella *adj* very.
Of course he's hella buff, he hits the gym at least three times a day.

hessian *n* a fan of heavy metal music.

hoochie *n* a promiscuous woman.

in your face *exc* blatantly aggressive exclamation used when embarrassing or upstaging someone, particularly in basketball.
Boo-yah! Did you see that dunk? In your face!

jack *v* to steal.

jack up *v* to inject drugs.

kick to the curb *v* to break up with someone.
They are not together anymore; she kicked him to the curb.

kicks *n* running shoes.

killer *adj* excellent; also very difficult.
OMG, that math test was killer.

legit *adj* legitimate, genuine, the real deal.

lowdown, the *n* the truth, inside info, unadulterated facts.

mega *adj* cool or fun; very.

merc *v* to kill.

mondo *adj* extremely; very large or great in amount or number.
That store has a mondo selection of nail polish colors.

my bad *exc* my mistake.
Sorry, I cut you off—my bad.

nabe *n* neighborhood.

off the hook very good, excellent; wild or crazy.

popo *n* the police.

posse *n* close group of friends; people with shared interests.

psych! *exc* retracts your statement; a way of saying "just kidding."
Since you're such a great friend, I got you a brand new car for your birthday—psych!

SLANG IN THE DIGITAL AGE
As e-mailing and text messaging became the preferred method of communication for many people, shortcuts or digital abbreviations for common phrases flourished. Here are a few of the more common ones:

B/C
Because

B4N
Bye for now

BF
Boyfriend

BFF
Best friends forever

BRB
Be right back

CUL8R
See you later

CWOT
Complete waste of time

DH
Dear husband

EOD
End of discussion

F2F
Face to face

FAQ
Frequently asked questions

FOFL
Falling on the floor laughing

FWIW
For what it's worth

FYI
For your information

G2G
Got to go

GF
Girlfriend

GR8
Great

ILY
I love you

IMHO
In my humble opinion

J4F
Just for fun

L8TR
Later

LOL
Laughing out loud

LMAO
Laughing my ass off

OMG
Oh my god

PLS
Please

PPL
People

RLY
Really

ROLF
Rolling on the floor laughing

SIT
Stay in touch

SUP
What's up?

TTYL
Talk to you later

WYSIWYG
What you see is what you get

VALLEY GIRL The 1980s saw a new suburban phenomenon emerge from California's San Fernando Valley area, the eponymous Valley Girl. Her singsongy, exclamation-heavy, up-talking style of speaking brought a wave of new slang into common usage.

AIRHEAD
An empty-headed person

AS IF
Exclamation, usually sarcastic, expressing disbelief

AWESOME
Excellent; really great

BARF ME OUT
Exclamation of disgust

DUH!
Comment on something perceived as stupid

DWEEB
An unattractive, socially awkward, or inept person

FOR SURE
Exclamation of agreement

GAG ME WITH A SPOON
Exclamation of disgust

GRODY
Disgusting

I'M SO SURE
Sarcastic response

LIKE
Interjected frequently between words for emphasis

SERIOUSLY
Interjection of agreement

TOTALLY
Interjection of approval

punked *v* humiliated; made the butt of a practical joke.

....

rad *adj* radical, excellent.

....

rag on *v* to insult or put someone down.
He's always ragging on the math teacher.

....

rock *v* to be great at something.
I rocked that speech.

....

salad dodger *n* an obese person.

....

scarf *v* to eat with great appetite and gusto.
That salad dodger just scarfed all the cupcakes.

....

shady *adj* suspicious, unnerving, either obvious or instinctual.

shred *v* to give a virtuoso performance in rock music, skateboarding, or surfing.
He totally shredded that song.

....

stylin' *adj* stylish, well-dressed.
She is so stylin'—I wish she'd be my personal shopper.

....

take a chill pill *exc* exhortation to relax or calm down.

....

talk to the hand *exc* phrase used to express a refusal to listen, usually accompanied by a hand gesture.
You jacked my kicks at the gym and now you want to be friends? Talk to the hand! EOD.

....

throw down *v* to fight.

....

veg out *adj* to relax; to spend time doing something that doesn't require too much thinking.

where's the beef? *exc* from a fast-food commercial, phrase used to imply something is lacking in substance.

....

wicked *adj* extremely cool, excellent.

....

wig out *v* to freak out.
My mom was wigging out about how late I came home last night, so I told her to take a chill pill.

....

yadda, yadda, yadda *exc* et cetera.
The lecturer just went on and on, yadda, yadda, yadda.

....

your mama *exc* an all-purpose insult or an expression of defiance; meant to incite rage in the target by way of their loyalty to their mother.

....

za *n* pizza.

GOOD-BYE

In the mid to late 20th century, there were many different ways to say "I'm out of here." These are a few of them:

Peace out

Let's book

Let's bounce

I'm gonna dip

Max out

Later

Gotta motor

Catch you on the flipside

Smell ya later

I'm gonna split

Ciao

I'm bailing

Deuces

Sayononara

Julie Tibbott is an editor of teen fiction at a major publishing house. Her interest in subcultures, history, and words inspired her to write *The Insult Dictionary*. Julie makes her home on New York City's Lower East Side.

Also Available
from Reader's Digest

Laughter, the Best Medicine @Work

Lighten up and laugh your way through the 9-to-5 grind with this mix of hilarious wisecracks, uproarious one-liners, full-color cartoons, and quotations from famous (and not-so-famous) wits. Whether you suffer from an e-mail gone wrong, an irritating coworker, or a dreadful boss, you'll see that laughter is the best medicine for all your work woes.

ISBN 978-1-60652-479-4 • $9.99 paperback

13 Things They Won't Tell You

From the wildly popular Reader's Digest column "13 Things," this book features more than 1,000 trade secrets for living smarter, richer, and happier. We asked hundreds of professionals in dozens of fields: What are the things you wish people knew? What should they know? What do you think they would be shocked to know? You won't believe what they said!

ISBN 978-1-60652-499-2 • $19.99 hardcover

Now That's Funny!

What do you get when you cross America's favorite magazine with the life work of an unapologetic joke thief? This book! In this rollicking collection, humor editor Andy Simmons has gathered the funniest jokes, interviews, essays, and anecdotes collected from the pages of Reader's Digest magazine, the oddest corner's of the country, and his own life.

ISBN 978-1-60652-500-5 • $14.99 paperback

Quotable Quotes: All New Wit & Wisdom
from the Greatest Minds of Our Time

The most well-known and succinct personalities of our time lend their memorable pearls of wit and wisdom—from comedians to scientists, from presidents to performers, from authors to athletes—to this updated edition of the best-selling book. Whether readers are looking to polish a speech, get a quick laugh, or be inspired by the wisdom of the world's greatest minds, Quotable Quotes will provide them with unique insights and revelatory perceptions.

ISBN 978-1-62145-004-7 • $14.99 hardcover

For more information, visit us at RDTradePublishing.com
E-book editions are also available.
Reader's Digest books can be purchased through retail and online bookstores.
In the United States books are distributed by Penguin Group (USA) Inc.
For more information or to order books, call 1-800-788-6262.